ABOUT THE AUTHOR

Ron Klug's interest in prayer, meditation, and the
practice of spiritual living began in college. He reads
the Bible regularly and continues to read great
devotional classics and modern expressions of Christian
prayer. For 25 years he has kept a journal and is the
author of *How to Keep a Spiritual Journal.* He is often
invited to speak on prayer, and to lead retreats and
address conferences.

Ron's spiritual life was deepened during a four-year
term as a missionary teacher in Madagascar. Prior to
his missionary experience, Ron taught elementary
school and college and was a book editor at Augsburg
Publishing House.

Now living in Northfield, Minnesota, with his wife
Lyn and their three children, Ron is a free-lance book
editor, magazine editor, speaker, and author.

He has written 22 books, including, *Growing in Joy;
You Promised, Lord; Lord, I've Been Thinking;* and
New Life for Men.

Ron and Lyn Klug coedited the popular *Christian
Family Bedtime Reading Book,* and are coauthors of
Bible Readings for Parents and five children's books—
*Jesus Lives; I'm a Good Helper; Please, God; Thank
You, God;* and *My Christmas ABC Book.*

BIBLE READINGS SERIES

Bible Readings for Women
  Lyn Klug

Bible Readings for Men
  Steve Swanson

Bible Readings for Couples
  Margaret and Erling Wold

Bible Readings for Singles
  Ruth Stenerson

Bible Readings for Families
  Mildred and Luverne Tengbom

Bible Readings for Parents
  Ron and Lyn Klug

Bible Readings for Teenagers
  Charles S. Mueller

Bible Readings for Students
  Ruth Stenerson

Bible Readings for Teachers
  Ruth Stenerson

Bible Readings for Church Workers
  Harry N. Huxhold

Bible Readings for the Retired
  Leslie F. Brandt

Bible Readings for Troubled Times
  Leslie F. Brandt

Bible Readings for Growing Christians
  Kevin E. Ruffcorn

Bible Readings for Farm Living
  Frederick Baltz

Bible Readings
ON PRAYER

Bible Readings

ON

PRAYER

•

Ron Klug

AUGSBURG Publishing House • Minneapolis

BIBLE READINGS ON PRAYER

Scripture quotations unless otherwise noted are from the Holy Bible: New International Version. Copyright 1978 by the New York International Bible Society. Used by permission of Zondervan Bible Publishers.

Scripture quotations marked TEV are from The Good News Bible, Today's English Version, copyright 1966, 1971, 1976 by American Bible Society. Used by permission.

Stanza 3 of the hymn "Thine Is the Kingdom" on p. 108 is copyright © Concordia Publishing House. Used by permission

Library of Congress Cataloging-in-Publication Data

Klug, Ron.
  BIBLE READINGS ON PRAYER.

  Bibliography: p.
  1. Prayer—Biblical teaching.   2. Prayers.
I. Title.
BS680.P64K55   1986   248.3'2   85-28979
ISBN 0-8066-2189-3

Manufactured in the U.S.A.   APH 10-0690

1 2 3 4 5 6 7 8 9 0 1 2 3 4 5 6 7 8 9

PREFACE

Whether you are a beginner in prayer, or whether you need to begin again, you are invited on a 100-day pilgrimage of prayer.

Each day you will read a portion of the Bible pertaining to prayer. I hope you will read the entire passage, and then concentrate on the key verse printed in this book. By the time you finish reading the book, you will have meditated on most of the Bible's key statements on prayer.

In the devotional reading for each day I have tried to share something of my own journey in prayer, as well as the experience of others. Along my way I have learned much from some of the great men and women of prayer, so I include some of their words. They represent many Christian traditions, but they are all part of God's family of prayer. At the end of this book I list some of their books that have helped me most.

The 100 readings have been arranged in a progression. We begin by looking at some of the basic biblical truths about prayer. Then we turn to the practical questions of when and where and how to pray. We examine some of the various types of prayer, like petition, intercession, confession, praise, and thanksgiving. We take up some difficulties in the life of prayer, and then close with the petitions of the Lord's Prayer as a summary of all we have learned on our journey.

After each reading is a prayer, which might serve best as a springboard to your own praying. Following this is a suggested action. These are important because we learn by doing—we learn to pray not just by reading about prayer, but by praying. Even though some of the actions may seem strange to you, I hope you will give them a try.

Although this book was written primarily for individual use, I hope it will also be helpful to prayer groups. A group or prayer circle could, for example, begin a meeting by reading one of the devotions and discussing the scripture text. If a group meets weekly, each member could read the devotion each day and perform the suggested action. When the group meets again, members could share their insights into Scripture and their experience of prayer.

A tool that might be useful with this book is a journal or notebook. Here you could write prayers and record your answers to prayer. You could copy in prayers you find. You could record your own questions or thoughts about prayer.

My prayer for you is that on this journey you will "grow in the grace and knowledge of our Lord and Savior Jesus Christ. To him be the glory, now and forever! Amen" (2 Peter 3:18 TEV).

■ TEACH US TO PRAY

Luke 11:1-4: "When he had finished, one of his disciples said to him, 'Lord, teach us to pray . . .'" (v. 1 TEV).

The only way we can live the Christian life is to underlay it with a life of prayer," wrote Constance Garrett in her book *Growth in Prayer*. One can no more live the Christian life without prayer than an electric light bulb can glow without being connected to a source of electricity. Garrett describes prayer as a "connecting cord which brings . . . the power of God into our lives so that we can glow with his light."

The disciples had already learned to say their prayers, yet the sight of Jesus at prayer prompted their request "Lord, teach us to pray." We, too, driven by our needs and drawn by the example of Jesus, depend on God to teach us to pray. Left to our own efforts, we would soon give up in frustration or laziness. We need God's help not only to learn *how* to pray, but to learn *to do it*.

Jesus welcomed the request of those first disciples, and he welcomes yours. He wants to teach you. We learn to pray by praying. Once we set our foot on the path, all the spiritual power of the universe is behind us and within us.

 Lord, teach me to pray.

Today make a commitment to yourself and to God that you will spend 100 days learning to pray.

■ COME BELIEVING

Hebrews 11: "Without faith it is impossible to please God, because anyone who comes to him must believe that he exists and that he rewards those who earnestly seek him" (v. 6).

Before we take up the practical topics regarding the how, when, and where of prayer, we need to look at some basic beliefs that undergird prayer. To begin to pray—or to continue—you don't need a theory of prayer. You don't even need to know much about God when you embark on the journey of prayer. It is enough to pray, like Walt Whitman, to "You whoever you are." You will learn more as you go—and the journey will go on into eternity.

Prayer can be thought of as original research, like an experiment. You don't need a formal hypothesis. It is enough to assume that God exists and that you can communicate with him, that God "rewards those who earnestly seek him." At this point in your life that conviction may not be very strong. That's all right. Just come to God with the faith you have. It may be as small as a mustard seed, but it has the power to move the mountains of doubt. As you study God's Word and pray, your faith will grow, because it has the power of God behind it.

 Lord God, I come with the faith I have. I believe you are there and that you will bless my seeking.

Today repeat to yourself several times: God is there, and he hears me.

■ CHOSEN

John 15:9-17: "You did not choose me, but I chose you to go and bear fruit—fruit that will last. Then the Father will give you whatever you ask in my name" (v. 16).

Prayer is so much more than an attempt to get blessings for ourselves. Whether we know it or not, we pray to sustain and deepen our relationship with God.

While it may seem that we are seeking God, it is really God who seeks us. You would not be seeking God if he had not already found you. You would not be interested in prayer if he were not calling you to pray. You speak to God because God has first spoken to you.

God always goes before you, giving you the desire to pray and teaching you to pray. This is one of the strongest incentives we have to pray—knowing that God loves us so much that he draws us to himself, that he has chosen us to bear fruit and that he promises to answer our prayer.

 Heavenly Father, I believe that you are drawing me into a deeper relationship with yourself through prayer.

Copy these words of St. Ignatius on a card and put it where you can see it often: "I come from God, I belong to God, I return to God."

■ THE SPIRIT PRAYS

Rom. 8:18-27: "In the same way, the Spirit helps us in our weakness. We do not know what we ought to pray, but the Spirit himself intercedes for us with groans that words cannot express" (v. 26).

In one sense prayer is something we do, but at a deeper level it is something God does in us and through us. If you feel, "I don't know how to pray" or "I don't know what to pray for," don't worry, because the Spirit of God prays for you and through you. Here is one of the great convictions of the Christian faith— that the Spirit of God is within us, to help us in our weakness. We are confronted with the mystery that God communicates with himself through us.

In this sense all prayer is the work of God's Spirit, a work of grace, a flame kindled by God. We pray because God gives us prayer.

We pray as best we can, even with "groans that words cannot express." And as we pray, the Spirit teaches us, one by one. You do not have to pray like anyone else. The Spirit will lead you into ways of prayer that are right for you.

 Come, Holy Spirit, kindle my heart and fill it with the fire of your love.

Remind yourself several times today: "The Spirit within is helping me pray."

■ IN EVERYTHING

Phil. 4:4-9: "Do not be anxious about anything, but in everything, by prayer and petition, with thanksgiving, present your requests to God" (v. 6).

Is it all right to pray for a parking place, for good weather, or for victory in a game? Should I trouble God with some of my "dumb" prayers? Is what I'm praying really right?

We need not be anxious about questions like this. If you are not sure if you should pray for something, do it anyway. "In everything . . . present your requests to God." Anything that concerns us concerns God and is a fit subject for prayer.

In his classic *Prayer* O. Hallesby wrote: "He knows that it is in our daily lives that we most easily become anxious. He knows, too, that our daily lives are made up of little things, not great things. Therefore he beckons us in a friendly way and says, 'Just bring all those little things to me, I am most willing to help you.' "

So we bring everything to God, trusting in his wisdom to sort it all out. We let him decide whether we are to receive what we ask for. We present our requests, knowing he will give us only what is good for us.

 O God of love and wisdom, I am grateful I can bring everything to you in prayer.

Is there anything you have hesitated to talk to God about? Pray about that today.

■ GOD IS NEAR

Psalm 145: "The Lord is near to all who call on him, to all who call on him in truth" (v. 18).

When one of the first Soviet astronauts returned from space, he announced that he had looked for God there but had not seen him. We think, "How foolish!" Yet we too may fall into the trap of thinking of God as far away—perhaps in a distant heaven.

Even though we do not always feel God's nearness, the Bible assures us that "he is not far from each one of us, 'For in him we live and move and have our being' " (Acts 17:27-28). God is "over all and through all and in all" (Eph. 4:6).

Gerhard Ebeling wrote: "To proclaim God as the God who is near, as Jesus did, is to put an end to the idea of heaven as God's distant dwelling place. . . . It is not that where heaven is, there is God, but rather where God is, there is heaven."

You pray to one who is as near as the depths of your own spirit.

 You are not a God who is far away, O Lord. I believe you are with me at this moment, and you will never abandon me.

Before you begin your time of prayer, take a few minutes to be quiet, to relax, to be still before God. Remind yourself, "God is near. God is with me. God is within me."

■ NOT MY WILL BUT YOURS

Mark 14:32-42: " '*Abba*, Father,' he said, 'everything is possible for you. Take this cup from me. Yet not what I will, but what you will' " (v. 36).

In *The World's Last Night* C. S. Lewis wrote, "There are, no doubt, passages in the New Testament which may seem at first sight to promise an invariable granting of our prayer. But that cannot be what they really mean. For in the very heart of the story we meet a glaring instance to the contrary. In Gethsemane the holiest of all petitioners prayed three times that a certain cup might pass from him. It did not. After that the idea that prayer is recommended to us as a sort of infallible gimmick may be dismissed."

While we can and should bring all our needs and desires to God, our prayer is not an attempt to bend God to our will, but to bend our will to his.

We know God's will in a general way. We know that God's will is love, that he wants peace and blessing and goodness for all. But when we pray, we often do not know God's will about specific matters. Therefore, we come, not demanding that God do our will, but humbly willing to submit to his will. We do not dictate how or when our prayer will be answered. It is enough to place the need before God and trust.

 Teach me to know and to trust your will for me, Lord God. In your will is my peace.

Memorize these words: "We know that in all things God works for the good of those who love him" (Rom. 8:28).

■ WAITING FOR GOD

Psalm 40:1-5:   "I waited patiently for the Lord's
help; then he listened to me and heard my cry"
(v. 1 TEV).

Ours is "The Instant Age." Instant coffee. Instant
potatoes. Instant winners. Instant intimacy. Instant
cash. Instant relief. It's no wonder that we expect
instant answers to prayer, and when God does not
provide them, prayer seems useless.

We do not always know why an answer to prayer is
delayed. It may be that we are not yet ready to
receive, or that God is preparing something even
better than we have asked for.

A great man of prayer, Leslie Weatherhead, left us
this realistic view in his book, *A Private House of
Prayer:* "I have always found prayer difficult. So often
it seems like a fruitless game of hide and seek in
which we seek and God hides. I know God is very
patient with me. Without that patience I should be
lost. But frankly I have to be patient with him. With
no other friend would I go on seeking with such scant,
conscious response. Yet I cannot leave prayer alone for
long. My need drives me to him. And I have a feeling
that he has his own reasons for hiding himself. And
that finally all my seeking will prove infinitely
worthwhile."

 God of Wisdom, teach me to trust your infinitely
wise timing.

**Have you ever had to wait for an answer to prayer?
What did you learn from the experience?**

■ ASK, SEEK, KNOCK

Matt.7:7-12: "Ask and it will be given to you; seek and you will find; knock and the door will be opened to you" (v. 7).

At times we all get discouraged about praying. We begin to wonder, does it really work? Does it do any good? Or we just don't feel like praying. At times like that it is good to remember two basic truths.

One, God has *commanded* us to pray. If we have no other reason to pray, we fall back on this. Prayer is not optional for the Christian. God says, "Ask, seek, knock." These are all imperatives. P. T. Forsyth went so far as to say, "The worst sin is prayerlessness." If you can think of no other reason to pray, pray because God tells you to pray.

Secondly, we pray because we have God's *promise*. To those who ask it will be given. Those who seek will find. Those who knock will find the door open for them. We who are parents enjoy giving gifts to our children. Even more does our Father in heaven. So we pray confidently, obeying God's command and trusting God's promise.

 Father in heaven, when I have doubts about prayer or when my desire fades, remind me of your command and your promise.

Write today's key verse on a card and carry it with you. Each time you think of it, stop and read it over.

■ A TIME TO PRAY

Psalm 55:   "Evening, morning and noon I cry out in distress, and he hears my voice" (v. 17).

If we are serious about learning to pray, we need to make time for it. While we can—and should—pray at all times, we also need a special time for prayer. I've found that when I schedule time for prayer, I am much more likely to carry prayer into the rest of the day.

Without a fixed time for prayer, we fall back on our fluctuating emotions, praying only when we feel like it. And the less we pray, the less we feel like praying. Conversely, the more we pray, the closer we grow to God and the more energy we have for prayer.

Hallesby wrote in his book *Prayer*, "All work takes time and when it becomes clear to us that prayer is a part of our daily program of work, it will also become clear to us that we must arrange our daily program in such a way that there is time also for this work."

Many of us already have bulging schedules, yet if we make time for even a few minutes of prayer each day, we will find that as we become more centered in God, we use all our time more efficiently and with greater blessing.

 Lord, teach me to take time to be in your healing and strengthening presence.

Think through your daily schedule. When can you set aside five or ten minutes for prayer? (Later you may want to extend this time.)

■ MORNING PRAYER

Mark 1:29-39: "Very early in the morning, while it was still dark, Jesus got up, left the house and went off to a solitary place, where he prayed" (v. 35).

The news of Jesus' healing Simon's mother-in-law spread quickly. By evening a great crowd of sick people were at the door, waiting for the healing touch of Jesus. Overwhelmed by the demands on his time and energy, Jesus needed to renew his contact with God. He dedicated the early morning hour to solitary prayer, and then was ready to return to his work of preaching and healing.

My days go best when I rise early enough to begin the day consciously in God's presence, seeking his guidance and strength for the day ahead. Someone has called this "praying the plotted day." Think through your day as far as you can predict it. Who will you be meeting? What will you be doing? What special challenges will you be facing? Who needs your help? Ask God's assistance for each task, each meeting, each anticipated joy, each relationship.

While it's easiest to do this sitting quietly in a chair or kneeling in a corner of your room, it can also be done in bed before you rise, or while washing up, or while riding the bus to work. However you do it, invite God into each portion of your day and look forward to God's guidance and strength.

 "Morning by morning, O Lord, you hear my voice; morning by morning I lay my requests before you and wait in expectation" (Ps. 5:3).

Tomorrow set time aside in the morning to pray "the plotted day."

■ EVENING PRAYER

Psalm 4: "I will lie down and sleep in peace, for you alone, O Lord, make me dwell in safety" (v. 8).

Each day can be enclosed in prayer. Begin by offering the day to God each morning and then review the day before you sleep. As you think back through the day, give thanks for each joy, each blessing, each experience of God's grace. Ask God's forgiveness for each failure to live up to his will, for each neglected opportunity to do good. Ask for his help in the struggles you faced that day. Then leave it all with God and "lie down and sleep in peace."

The spiritual writers of the ages have stressed the importance of the last few waking minutes. The thoughts we choose to entertain at that time are carried into the subconscious and continue to work even while we are asleep. Martin Luther made this recommendation: "At night always carry in your heart something from the Holy Scriptures to bed with you, meditate upon it, like a ruminant animal, and go softly to sleep. But this must not be too much—rather a little that may be well-pondered and understood, that you may find a remnant of it in your mind when you rise in the morning."

 Let my last thoughts each night be of you and your love for me, O Lord.

Tonight review your day in God's presence. Try Luther's suggestion and repeat the words of Psalm 4:8 as you prepare for sleep.

■ GRACE AT MEALS

Luke 24:28-35: "When he was at the table with them, he took bread, gave thanks, broke it and began to give it to them" (v. 30).

On the first Easter Jesus stopped at the home of those Emmaus disciples for the evening meal, and it was not until he took the bread and gave thanks that they were aware of God's presence with them.

Whether you eat alone or with others, mealtime is a natural time to pray. The food on the table reminds us of our dependence on God and moves us to give thanks. We are also reminded of the hungry and needy throughout the world, and we bring them into our prayer.

As we receive food for our body, each meal can recall our need for spiritual food. God feeds our spirits through the Word and the sacraments. And as we are fed now, we look forward to the even closer relationship with God in heaven, a relationship so close and so joyous that the Bible speaks of it as a banquet.

Dietrich Bonhoeffer wrote in *Life Together*, "The fellowship of the table teaches Christians that here they still eat the perishable bread of the earthly pilgrimage. But if they shall share this bread with one another, they shall also one day receive the imperishable bread together in the Father's house."

 Lord of life, as I receive food for my body, let me look forward to the heavenly banquet of life eternal in your presence.

Take time at each meal to thank God for your blessings and to pray for the world's hungry.

■ IN THE WATCHES OF THE NIGHT

Psalm 119:145-152:   "My eyes stay open through the watches of the night, that I may meditate on your promises" (v. 148).

Everybody at the retirement center complains at breakfast about how little sleep they got and how long the night was," 83-year-old Hilda reported. "Not me. If I'm awake at night, I just use the time for prayer. Either I pray for all the people I know who need help, or I just take a Bible verse I have memorized and repeat it over and over slowly to myself. The night passes quickly, and in the morning I feel well-rested."

I normally sleep very well, but for a time I was troubled by insomnia. I fussed over this until I realized this was an answer to my need for quiet time for reflection and prayer.

The psalm writer must have had a similar experience. It can be yours too. Like Hilda, you may want to quietly lift friends and family members up to God, praying that his will be done in the life of each one. Or take a reassuring Bible verse and repeat it softly. St. Francis is reported to have prayed the whole night the simple prayer, "My Lord and my God."

 O God of peace and comfort, help me remember you in the watches of the night.

Make a list of five Bible verses you could use as prayers in the night.

■ CONTINUAL PRAYER

1 Thess. 5:12-28: "Be joyful always; pray
continually; give thanks in all circumstances"
(vv. 16-18).

Set times of prayer enable us to pray throughout the
day. This does not mean, of course, that we are
expressing words of prayer at every moment. We
could hardly do that and complete the other tasks God
sets before us. But it is possible for us to make prayer
a part of all we do.

This action of praying at all times is one answer to
the common cry, "I just don't have enough time!" All
of us have spare minutes, "crumbs of wasted time," in
which to turn to God without interrupting the flow of
our work or conversation. At first we may be able to
do this only a few minutes each day, but as we grow
accustomed to it, we will find it a natural response,
almost like walking or breathing.

We can develop the habit of praying each time we
make a telephone call or meet a client. When we
write a letter, we can pray for the one addressed. As
we push the cart down the supermarket aisle, we can
thank God for his provision. Luther wrote: "There is
no Christian who does not have time to pray without
ceasing . . . no one is so heavily·burdened with his
labor, but that if he will he can, while working, speak
with God in his heart, lay before him his need and
that of other men, ask for help, make petition, and in
all this exercise and strengthen his faith."

 O Holy Spirit, help me make prayer part of the
fabric of my whole life.

**Today make a special effort to use "crumbs of wasted
time" for prayer.**

■ A PLACE TO PRAY

Matt. 6:5-6: "When you pray, go into your room, close the door and pray to your Father, who is unseen. Then your Father, who sees what is done in secret, will reward you" (v. 6).

We have seen some of the Bible's answers to the question, *When* should we pray? Now let us look briefly at, *Where* shall we pray?

Because we are creatures with a body and much influenced by habit, it helps to have a special corner or a room where we pray regularly. Ideally we should have a chair that is comfortable, but not so plush that we drowse off. A cross or picture of Jesus can focus our thoughts. A Bible or book of prayers may be at hand. Probably most important is to have space where we can be uninterrupted, free from noise.

It may be best if you can create a special place of prayer in your own home or room, but not all of us have the luxury of private space. Those who do not could consider praying in a church or a park or other setting that provides solitude and silence. Whatever the place, go there regularly to meet God.

 Creator God, help me find a good place for my time with you.

Do something today to create or find a special place where you can pray undisturbed.

■ ANY PLACE WILL DO

John 4:19-23: "Believe me, woman, a time is coming when you will worship the Father neither on this mountain nor in Jerusalem" (v. 21).

Perhaps this woman was sincerely plagued by the question, Where is the proper place to worship? Maybe she was just changing the subject to dodge Jesus' inquiries into her life. At any rate, Jesus' answer was that worship need not be limited to "sacred" space like a church. "True worship finds God in every place," wrote William Barclay.

When I was learning to write, I found it easiest to have a set time and place. Since then I have written on trains, in airports, bus depots, and public parks. In learning to pray, we may need a special place, but then we develop the ability to pray freely wherever we are. Jesus prayed in the Garden of Gethsemane. Paul prayed aboard ship. Peter prayed in jail.

When Jacob was fleeing from his brother Esau, he slept in a desert place with only a stone for a pillow. The Lord appeared to him in a dream, and when Jacob awoke, he thought, "Surely the Lord is in this place, and I was not aware of it" (Gen. 28:16). God is present in all places ready to meet us. We need only reach out toward him.

 You are present in every place, O Lord. Help me to realize your presence here and now.

Today try praying some place where you do not ordinarily pray. Begin with Jacob's words.

■ PRAY WITH YOUR BODY

Rom. 12:1-2: ". . . offer your bodies as living
sacrifices, holy and pleasing to God—which is your
spiritual worship" (v. 1).

We begin now to look at the question, *How* should
we pray?

Today we are learning to think holistically—to
consider the whole person. We know that we do not
worship God only with our minds or with some part
called *spirit* or *soul*. We worship God also with our
bodies.

The Bible describes many postures for prayer.
Daniel kneeled. David sat. Ezekiel prostrated himself
face-down. Jesus looked up to heaven when he
prayed. The tax collector beat his breast to show
sorrow for sin. Paul spoke of lifting up holy hands in
prayer. Some Christians make the sign of the cross
when they pray.

Actions like these are not required. God does not
need them, but you may find them helpful. There may
even be times when we are too exhausted to pray in
words, but can only kneel as a sign of our submission
to God.

God loves all of you; God wants all of you. You can
pray also with your body.

 Creator God, thank you for the gift of my body.
Today I offer it to you as part of my spiritual
worship.

**How can you pray to God with your body? Choose
one way and practice it today.**

■ TAKE WORDS

Hosea 14: "Take words with you and return to the Lord" (v. 2).

Most of us have learned that we don't need special "religious" language in order to pray, for example, the language of Shakespeare's England. Yet the words we use in prayer are important, and they can be a problem. What kind of words should we take with us when we return to the Lord?

At times words that express just what we mean come spontaneously. Then the language of prayer is no problem. But at other times we find it difficult to put our deepest yearnings into words, or our words seem empty or insincere. At such times we may be helped by using the words of others—the Psalms, a great hymn, a poem, or a prayer of some stalwart Christian of the past or present. Written prayers can also deepen and extend the range of our prayer life.

In *Beginning to Pray*, Anthony Bloom gives good advice: "The first act of prayer is to choose such words as are completely true to what you are, words which you are not ashamed of, which express you adequately and are worthy of you—and then offer them to God with all the intelligence of which you are capable."

 Holy Spirit, lead me to the prayers I need to express my truest and deepest thoughts to you.

Today begin a notebook in which you write prayers you find that can deepen and enrich your prayer life.

■ HONEST PRAYER

Psalm 44:   "Awake, O Lord! Why do you sleep?
Rouse yourself! Do not reject us forever" (v. 23).

In *Letters to Malcolm: Chiefly on Prayer* C. S. Lewis
wrote, "It is no use to ask God with factitious
earnestness for A when our whole mind is in reality
filled with the desire for B. We must lay before Him
what is in us, not what ought to be in us."

Sometimes what is in us is not very nice. We might
feel like "patient" Job: "You have worn me out, God;
you have let my family be killed. You have seized me;
you are my enemy" (Job 16:7 TEV). Or like Jesus on
the cross, "My God, my God, why have you forsaken
me?" (Mark 15:34).

The psalm writers were honest to God in their
prayers. There's no sense pretending we are cheery
when we are depressed, loving when we are spiteful,
trusting when we are in doubt. Better to express what
we really feel—after all, God knows anyway. Once
those feelings are acknowledged, God can begin to
change them. Having spoken honestly to God, we can
say, "Rise up and help us; redeem us because of your
unfailing love" (Psalm 44:26).

 O God of truth, help me to be truthful in what I
pray.

**What feelings or thoughts are hardest for you to offer
to God? Think about that, and then pray about those
things today in the spirit of the psalmist.**

■ A TIME FOR SILENCE

Psalm 37:1-9: "Be still before the Lord and wait patiently for him" (v. 7).

An old peasant who spent many hours sitting in church was asked, "What do you do there all those hours?" He answered, "I look at God, and he looks at me, and we are happy."

There is a time in prayer for silence, a time to be still before the Lord. Old friends or people who have been married a long time are often comfortable in one another's presence without talking. They are able to communicate at a level deeper than words.

Hallesby wrote: "It is not necessary to maintain a conversation when you are in the presence of God. We can come into his presence and rest our weary souls in quiet contemplation of Him. Our groanings, which cannot be uttered, rise to Him and tell Him better than words how dependent we are upon Him."

 Lord, in the midst of my noisy world, let me know and experience the blessing of silent prayer.

Now take a few minutes and sit quietly with the thought: "I am in God's presence. I will be still."

■ PRAYER AND THE WORD

John 15:1-8: "If you remain in me and my words remain in you, ask whatever you wish and it will be given to you" (v. 7).

Jesus here lays down two conditions for prayer. We are to remain in Jesus, like a branch in a vine, drawing our spiritual life from him. And his words are to remain in us.

Prayer is not meant to be a monolog in which we do all the talking. Prayer should include a time when we listen to God. We might begin our time of prayer by reading from the Bible or some spiritual book based on the Bible. As we read, we might ask ourselves three questions: What does this teach me about God? What does this teach me about myself? Is there something here that I need to do?

The Word informs our prayer, giving us the mind of Christ. Perhaps that is why Jesus linked his words with the promise, "Ask whatever you wish, and it will be given to you." If Jesus' words remain in you, your mind will be so formed that you will ask only for that which it is God's will to give you.

 Lord Jesus, I want to remain in you. May your words remain in me.

If you are not already doing so, establish a plan for regular Bible reading. You may want to start with the Gospels in the New Testament or the Psalms in the Old Testament.

■ MEDITATION AND PRAYER

Psalm 104:24-35: "May my meditation be pleasing to him, as I rejoice in the Lord" (v. 34).

For many, *meditation* is still a strange word. Some associate it more with Buddhism or Hinduism than with Christianity. Yet meditation is a good biblical word. The Bible encourages us to meditate on God's Word and works. While the word *meditation* does not occur in the New Testament, the idea is there: "Mary treasured up all these things and pondered them in her heart" (Luke 2:19); "Finally, brothers, whatever is true, whatever is noble, whatever is right, whatever is pure, whatever is lovely, whatever is admirable—if anything is excellent or praiseworthy—think about such things" (Phil. 4:8).

Meditation in its simplest form is thinking about God, reminding ourselves of the truths we already know about God, maybe even arguing ourselves away from moments of unbelief back toward faith. Our meditation will often grow naturally from our spiritual reading, especially if we learn to take one thought from the reading and ponder it during the day. Meditation is an excellent preparation for prayer. We move naturally from thinking about God to talking to God.

 "May the words of my mouth and the meditation of my heart be pleasing in your sight, O Lord, my Rock and my Redeemer" (Ps. 19:14).

If you want to learn more about Christian meditation, read Morton Kelsey's book *The Other Side of Silence* (Paulist, 1976).

31

■ THE DART PRAYER

Matt. 14:25-32:   "But when he saw the wind, he was afraid and, beginning to sink, cried out, 'Lord, save me!' " (v. 30).

For Peter there was no time for theological debate or a lengthy pious prayer. There was time only for a hasty cry from the very center of his life, "Lord, save me!"

Our lives provide us with many opportunities for such "dart" or "flash" prayers. They come naturally in times of crisis, when we cry out for the Lord's help. But these can also be prayers: a quick upward look of adoration, the loving repetition of the name of Jesus, the lifting up of the heart in gratitude. In the midst of life momentary prayers like these help keep us aware of God.

These brief prayers can be for others too. Frank Laubach, literacy pioneer and man of prayer, wrote in *Prayer: The Mightiest Force in the World*, "From now on, you must never fail to pray whenever you think of it, if only for a second. . . . Our prayer seems to be weak at first, but as we practice with thousands upon thousands of these flash prayers, we feel them come back to us like radar. When that happens, our hearts skip a beat with the thrill of it, for we know we are learning to be channels for God, and what is more, that we are children of God, working with Him for His Kingdom."

 Spirit of life, remind me to pray often during each day.

Today pray whenever you think of it.

■ PRAYER PARTNERS

Matt. 18:15-20:   "Again, I tell you that if two of you
on earth agree about anything you ask for, it will be
done for you by my Father in heaven" (v. 19).

Perhaps most of our time in prayer is rightly spent
alone with God. But there are also benefits in praying
with one other person or a small group. For one thing,
it is a discipline; when we have made an appointment
with others, we tend to keep that appointment. We
also learn how to pray from one another. Because
there is always the possibility of selfishness and self-
delusion in prayer, others help us determine whether
what we are praying is according to God's will.
When our own prayer falters, we are upheld and
strengthened by the confidence of our prayer partners.
At times we may even be so weak or depressed that
we cease praying and allow ourselves to rest in the
prayers of others.
    Jesus encourages small-group prayer by promising
God's blessing and by assuring us that God is with the
two or three who gather in his name.

 Lord, lead me to those with whom I can pray
and those who need me to pray with them.

**If you do not now regularly pray with others,
consider asking one or two friends to meet regularly
for prayer, or join an already existing prayer group.**

■ PUBLIC PRAYER

Psalm 111: "I will extol the Lord with all my heart in the council of the upright and in the assembly" (v. 1).

The great Anglican spiritual writer Evelyn Underhill wrote: "I feel the regular, steady, docile practice of corporate worship is of the utmost importance for the building-up of your spiritual life. . . . no amount of solitary reading makes up for humble immersion in the life of the worship of the church."

Solitary prayer, small-group prayer, and the public worship of the church—three legs of a stool. We are social beings, and so a comprehensive life of prayer includes prayer with others.

Certain actions or attitudes may enrich our public worship. Instead of focusing on what we "get" out of church, we can think of going there to offer the worship we owe to God. Instead of criticizing the preacher or the choir, we can pray for them. If our congregation uses a regular system of Bible readings, we can read them ahead of time. Even getting enough sleep the night before is a help, as is arriving at church early enough to become settled in mind and spirit. All these may enable us to say with sincerity, "I rejoiced with those who said to me, 'Let us go to the house of the Lord' " (Ps. 122:1).

 O God of all, thank you for the freedom we have to worship you together. Help me appreciate this blessing.

What can you do to make your public worship a more blessed experience?

■ WHAT DO YOU WANT?

Matt. 20:32: "Jesus stopped and called them.
'What do you want me to do for you?' he asked."

As Jesus left Jericho, over the noise of the crowd
came the shout, "Lord, Son of David, have mercy on
us." Jesus responded to that cry for mercy with a
question. He asked them to be specific: "What do you
want me to do for you?" The blind men answered,
"Lord, we want our sight."

It may help us to be specific in our prayers—not
that God needs to know, but definite prayer teaches
us to understand our own needs better. This may take
time and self-scrutiny.

We should not despise our own wants. They may be
clues to God's will for us. In *Prayer in Other Words*
Dom Hubert von Zeller explains, "God has certain
things in store for us which he knows we need and
which he means to give us. But he means to give
them only on condition that we ask for them. So he
fills our mind with a desire for these things and gives
us grace to turn our desire into a prayer for them."

 Lord Jesus, I thank you for all good desires—
that you give them and that you are ready to
fulfill them.

**Right now imagine Jesus standing in front of you. He
asks, "What do you want me to do for you?" How do
you answer him?**

■ ALL YOUR NEEDS

Phil. 4:10-20: "And my God will meet all your needs according to his glorious riches in Christ Jesus" (v. 19).

God has promised to meet all our needs, but not necessarily all our greeds. For example, God will meet our need for companionship, but the people he sends may not be glamorous or talented. One of our great tasks is to determine our true needs. They may be far fewer than advertisers want us to believe.

Ask God to show you your real needs. So often we think we need one thing, but then we get it and find it is not what we needed at all. We can be sure we don't *need* anything contrary to God's will. We may want it, but we don't need it. God, who made us, knows our true needs—and is always working to meet them.

And then, because God loves us, he not only meets our needs, but blesses us in ways we have not even imagined.

I am trusting you to guide me;
You alone shall lead,
Every day and hour supplying
All my need.

Personalize the promise of Phil. 4:19. Repeat to yourself: "And with all his abundant wealth through Christ Jesus, God will supply all my needs."

■ DECISION MAKING

Acts 1:15-26:   "Lord, you know everyone's heart.
Show us which of these two you have chosen"
(v. 24).

The Bible contains many examples of believers who
sought God's help when they faced a decision. When
Eliezer had to travel to find a wife for Isaac, he asked
God's help in recognizing the right woman. Samuel
asked God's help in knowing which of Jesse's sons to
anoint as king. David often inquired of the Lord
before he made a decisive move. The apostles asked
God's help in choosing a successor to replace Judas.

To determine God's will, the apostles cast lots. It
seems that in both Old and New Testaments believers
often used what look like games of chance to
determine God's will. We probably look less to such
means and more to God's inner guidance. We can
request God's guidance for all the decisions of life—
not only major ones like the choice of a career or a
spouse, but also in the daily details of home life and
business.

In most cases God's answer will come in some
unspectacular way. And if we misread the signals, God
can forgive us and lead us to correct our mistake. The
important thing is to ask. When we pray, "Lord, what
do you want me to do?" God will answer.

 Holy Spirit, I look to you for guidance in all my
decision making.

**Is there a decision you are facing right now? Ask
God's help and trust that God's guidance will be
coming.**

■ NOT TO WORRY

Matt. 6:25-34: "But seek first his kingdom and his righteousness, and all these things will be given to you as well. Therefore do not worry about tomorrow, for tomorrow will worry about itself. Each day has enough trouble of its own" (vv. 33-34).

There are some simple ideas that it takes a lifetime to learn. One I'm working on is "one day at a time." I find myself worrying about what my ten-year-old will be like when he's a teenager instead of enjoying him today. I worry about a deadline I have to meet three months from now instead of concentrating on the work I have to do today. I'm trying to learn how to live in "day-tight compartments," without resentment over the past or worries about tomorrow.

We do have a choice. We can choose to worry or we can choose to live today as well as we can, entrusting tomorrow to God. Dom Hubert von Zeller suggests the right attitude: "God *loves* the world and every soul in it. Why should we break our heads worrying about either our own future or the future of the world?"

Jesus is the one who bids me not to worry about tomorrow, and he is teaching me to leave those worries with him.

 Lord Jesus, help me live each day well and leave the future with you.

Complete this sentence: Just for today I will . . . .

■ THE NAME OF JESUS

John 14:5-14: "You may ask me for anything in my name, and I will do it" (v. 14).

I have a friend who is a librarian in a city near where I live. I don't have a library card for that library, but he lets me use his. I can check out all the books and records I want *in his name*.

Praying "in Jesus' name" does not mean just tacking on that phrase at the end of each prayer. It means understanding that I come before God, not on my own merits, but on his. In that sense all Christian prayer is in the name of Jesus.

More than that, in the Bible *name* means the nature or character of a person. To pray in Jesus' name is to pray in accord with his nature, in harmony with his will as we know it. We cannot pray for things he would disapprove of. We cannot pray for something that wounds someone else. Our prayers must be in Jesus' name, and that name is Love.

The test of any prayer, then, is "Can I honestly pray this in the name of Jesus?" One reason for reading the Gospels regularly is that we will come to know Jesus so well that we will know the answer to that question. Then we have the confidence that a prayer asked in his name will be granted, because it is his will.

 Lord Jesus, I am thankful that I can pray in your name.

If you're not sure of a prayer, ask yourself, "Can I pray this in Jesus' name? Is this a prayer Jesus would pray?"

■ PRAYER OF SUBMISSION

Heb. 5:1-10: "He offered up prayers and petitions with loud cries and tears to the one who could save him from death, and he was heard because of his reverent submission" (v. 7).

Jesus, we're told by the writer of Hebrews, prayed to one who could save him from death—and he was heard. But that did not mean God spared him from death. Jesus submitted to death, accepting in Gethsemane the will of the Father, and God led him beyond death to the triumph of the resurrection.

For us, too, victory in prayer may sometimes come through submission to the will of God. Sometimes it seems as if our own tension, our own steely will, blocks God's answer, and it is only when we become pliant and yielding that we can receive what God wants to give. We have to be willing to let go, if that seems to be God's intention. One of my favorite hymns expresses this confidence in God's love and wisdom.

> *What God ordains is always good;*
> *his will abideth holy.*
> *As He directs my life for me,*
> *I follow meek and lowly.*
> *My God indeed In every need*
> *Doth well know how to shield me;*
> *To Him, then, I will yield me.*

 Jesus, your prayers were heard because you submitted to God's will. Help me learn from you.

Is there some situation in which your prayer has been demanding or frustrated? Today, by an act of will, say, "Lord, I relinquish this to you. Help me believe that all things will work together for my good."

■ BEFORE YOU ASK

Isaiah 65: "Before they call I will answer; while they are still speaking I will hear" (v. 24).

Isaiah gives us a glorious picture of the new age, the age of the Messiah. The relationship between God and believers will then be so close that God will answer a prayer while the person is still speaking. St. Augustine wrote: "God does not ask us to tell him our needs that he may learn about them, but in order that we may be capable of receiving what he is preparing to give."

At times we experience an almost instantaneous answer to prayer. At other times, it is as if God immediately sends the answer winging on its way toward us, but it takes a while before circumstances or our own heart is such that we can receive the answer.

We do not need to bombard God with information. We do not need to break down some thick wall of indifference between us and God. P. T. Forsyth wrote: "Love loves to be told what it knows already; it wants to be asked for what it longs to give."

 Lord God, I thank you for the reassuring word that even while I am praying, you are already answering.

As you begin your time of prayer, picture Jesus saying to you, "Before you call I will answer. While you are still speaking I will hear."

■ IMMEASURABLY MORE

Eph. 3:14-21: "Now to him who is able to do immeasurably more than all we ask or imagine, according to his power that is at work within us . . ." (vv. 20-21).

How often our prayers are timid, safe, predictable. We pray small prayers because we are afraid God can't handle the big ones or because we feel God is too busy to bother with us. Or we think of God as helpless to do anything for us.

The prayer that Paul prayed for the Ephesians is a mind-expander, a faith-builder. He prays that God may strengthen you with power through his Spirit in your inner being, "that Christ may dwell in your hearts through faith," that you may be "rooted and established in love." He especially asks that we might have the power to grasp the extent of Christ's love, that we might be filled "to the measure of all the fulness of God." Let those phrases sink deeply into your mind and spirit.

When those phrases take hold of us, we will pray bold prayers, knowing that we have no weak, helpless God, but one who is "able to do so much more than we can ever ask for, or even think of: to God be the glory in the church and in Christ Jesus for all time, forever and ever! Amen" (Eph. 3:20-21 TEV).

 O God of might, open my mind to grasp the depth of your love and the greatness of your power at work within me.

Think of the three boldest prayers you could pray. Pray them now.

■ WITH ALL YOUR HEART

Jer. 29:10-14: "You will seek me and find me when you seek me with all your heart" (v. 13).

A young man came to a spiritual teacher and said, "I want to know God." The teacher took the seeker down to a river and forced his head under water. The young man struggled until he finally came up gasping. The teacher said, "When you want God as much as you wanted air, you will find him." God says, "You will seek me and find me when you seek me with all your heart" (Jer. 29:13).

We seek God because God has summoned us. God draws us to himself even through our most imperfect, even selfish, prayers. Louis Evely wrote in *The Prayer of Modern Man*, "Everyone who prays begins by asking for something that he wants, something that he has set his heart on; but if he prays truly, by the time he has finished he will have set his heart not on the thing he was asking for but on Him of whom he was asking it."

 Lord, it is not what you can give me that I want, but you yourself.

Memorize today's promise. Repeat it often as you go about your day.

■ ACCORDING TO HIS WILL

1 John 5:13-15: "This is the assurance we have in approaching God: that if we ask anything according to his will, he hears us. And if we know that he hears us—whatever we ask—we know that we have what we asked of him" (vv. 14-15).

In *The Struggle of Prayer* Donald Bloesch wrote, "We glorify God by seeking to know his will, by beseeching him to declare his will to us. We also glorify God when we seek his aid to accomplish his will."

How do we determine God's will? We believe that in the Bible God has revealed his will, so Bible reading always has an important place in our prayer. God also continues to reveal his will through the church, the fellowship of believers. Sometimes God's will is revealed through circumstances, as God brings people or events into our lives. God's will also is revealed through the gifts God has given us. If God has bestowed a certain talent, as in art or business, we can be sure that he wants us to develop that gift and use it for his glory and to benefit others.

When you are sure that what you are asking is in line with God's will, then you can pray with confidence so sure that it is as if you already have what you ask of God.

 Lord, I believe that if I honestly seek to know your will, you will reveal it to me. Then I can pray with confidence.

If there's a situation in which you are not sure about God's will, talk it over with another Christian you trust.

■ NEVER GIVE UP

Luke 11:5-10: "I tell you, though he will not get up and give him the bread because he is his friend, yet because of the man's persistence he will get up and give him as much as he needs" (v. 8).

During the depths of World War II, when London suffered under German bombardment and the fate of Europe hung in the balance, Winston Churchill was asked to speak to a group of British school boys. He stepped before them with the briefest of speeches: "Never give up. Never give up. Never. Never. Never."

Jesus told the parable of the friend at midnight to make one point: that persistent prayer is sure of an answer. We should not push the parable too far. God is not like the lazy friend, who gives bread just to silence the beggar. Why God delays an answer to prayer is usually a mystery to us. Perhaps we are being taught to trust God, to detach our faith from self-reliance or our own judgment. Perhaps it has to do with our readiness to receive God's blessing. At any rate, we can trust that God will not delay one moment longer than is necessary.

C. S. Lewis said it this way: "God keeps no one waiting unless He sees that it is good for him to wait."

 Lord, give me the grace to persist in prayer.

When you're tempted to stop praying, remember Winston Churchill!

■ IF YOU BELIEVE

Matt. 21:18-22: "If you believe, you will receive whatever you ask for in prayer" (v. 22).

We now come to the essential, but difficult, topic of faith and prayer. Jesus says plainly that if we believe and do not doubt, we can receive whatever we ask for. We can make a fig tree wither or can even move mountains. Immediately the questions come: Is he exaggerating for effect? Does the promise apply only to those spiritual giants who have reached a high plateau of faith? Why do so many prayers seem to go unanswered?

Our temptation is probably to dismiss this promise too quickly because it threatens to set us up for defeat or seems to demand more faith of us than we have.

Later we will see that the Bible gives reasons why our prayers are sometimes not granted, and we must place this verse in the context of everything else the Bible tells us about prayer. But for now, live with these words of Jesus. Let them open your heart and enlarge your vision. Let them awaken in you a desire for greater faith and give you a larger awareness of God's power and willingness to answer believing prayer.

 Don't let me trim this promise to the level of my own unbelief, O Lord. May it instead open my mind and quicken my faith.

Before you begin today, repeat this promise ten times. Then think of your special needs and the needs of others and bring them before God in faith.

■ HELP OF THE HELPLESS

Matt. 19:16-26:   "With man this is impossible, but with God all things are possible" (v. 26).

Sometimes we find ourselves in situations where we feel helpless—helpless to know how to pray or to summon up the faith that God will answer prayer. It is just then that we need to pray.

Hear the assuring words of Hallesby: "Be not anxious because of your helplessness. Above all, do not let it prevent you from praying. Helplessness is the real secret and the impelling power of prayer. You should therefore rather try to thank God for the feeling of helplessness which he has given you. It is one of the greatest gifts which God can impart to us. For it is only when we are helpless that we open our hearts to Jesus and let Him help us in our distress, according to his grace and mercy. Prayer is just telling God the ways in which we are helpless."

Then we ask God to lift our eyes beyond our helplessness to God's power. With God all things are possible.

 "Help of the helpless, oh, abide with me."

What is the most difficult situation or problem you face? Remind yourself, "For me this is impossible, but with God all things are possible."

■ INCREASE MY FAITH

Mark 9:14-29: "I do believe; help me overcome my unbelief!" (v. 24).

The disciples could not heal this boy, Jesus said, because they were part of an "unbelieving generation." The father had only a tentative faith: "If you can do anything . . ." he said. Only Jesus had unconquerable faith: "Everything is possible for him who believes." And with that faith Jesus healed the boy.

We are often like that father, our faith weak and fragile, and we can learn from him. Though there be little faith and much doubt in our hearts, we can still bring our need before Jesus. We can honestly tell him of our doubts and the weakness of our faith, and we can pray, "I do have faith, but not enough. Help me have more!" (Mark 9:24 TEV).

Let us be clear: it is not faith in prayer we need. It is not faith in faith. It is faith in God. A.W. Tozer gave us this definition: "Faith is the gaze of a soul upon a saving God."

 Spirit of life, I know I cannot create this faith in myself. It can only be your gift. Increase my faith.

Think back over your prayers of the past weeks. Is there some situation about which you're praying where you need more confidence? Ask God to increase your faith.

■ STANDING ON THE PROMISES

Psalm 145: "The Lord is faithful to all his promises
and loving toward all he has made" (v. 13).

When his good friend and co-worker Philipp
Melanchthon was seriously ill, Luther went to the
throne of grace boldly to seek healing for him: "This
time I besought the Almighty with great vigor. I
attacked him with his own weapons, quoting from
Scripture all the promises I could remember, that
prayers should be granted, and said that he must grant
my prayer, if I was henceforth to put faith in his
promises."

Luther teaches us to hang our faith on the clear
promises of Scripture. Among the hundreds of
promises in the Bible, these are some of my favorites:

"I can do everything through him who gives me
strength" (Phil. 4:13).

"I will instruct you and teach you in the way you
should go; I will counsel you and watch over you" (Ps.
32:8).

"And we know that in all things God works for the
good of those who love him" (Rom. 8:28).

Prayer becomes more possible for us when we learn
to know and to trust God's promises.

 Lord God, thank you for your promises and
your faithfulness.

**Begin a list of the biblical promises that mean the
most to you. Add to the list from time to time.
Commit the promises to memory and use them in
your prayers.**

■ BUILD YOURSELF UP

Jude 20: "But you, dear friends, build yourselves up in your most holy faith and pray in the Holy Spirit."

The Bible is clear that faith is necessary for effective prayer. We have seen that faith is a gift of God for which we should pray. Faith for prayer cannot be separated from our whole spiritual life. The closer we are to God, the more we know of God, the more we allow God to have his way in our lives, the more we dedicate our lives to God, the greater will be our faith.

We build ourselves up in the faith by learning more about God through Bible study and spiritual reading. We grow in faith as we associate with people of faith, people of prayer. And prayer itself builds faith.

One way we can build ourselves up in the faith is to write out our prayers. A missionary friend keeps a record of her prayers, writing down a definite petition and the date on which it was first made. Then she records how God answered the prayer and the date. By reviewing the answers to prayer, she is strengthened in faith and motivated to pray.

 Lord, help me do those things that build my faith.

Try writing down your prayers and keeping a record of God's answers.

■ THE GIFT OF THE SPIRIT

Luke 11:9-13: "If you then, though you are evil, know how to give good gifts to your children, how much more will your Father in heaven give the Holy Spirit to those who ask him!" (v. 13).

The idea seems deeply imbedded in us that we have to try to wring gifts out of God, that we need to win his favor, to strike a bargain with him. Or we try to work ourselves up to an intensity of faith or feeling in the hope that our prayer will be more effective. All that is unnecessary. Years ago Archbishop Trench said, "We must not conceive prayer as an overcoming of God's reluctance, but a laying hold of his highest willingness."

Of all the good things God is willing to give, the highest gift is the Spirit, a gift given to the degree that we are open to receive. We may resist the coming of the Spirit, because the Spirit's coming is costly to us. It may mean fighting against pet sins, reordering our priorities, or changing habitual actions. To open ourselves to the Spirit is to be open to God's transforming power. When God comes he produces in us this fruit: "love, joy, peace, patience, kindness, goodness, faithfulness, gentleness and self-control" (Gal. 5:22). To pray is to desire these things and to be willing to let go of all that opposes them.

 Father in heaven, you long to give me good gifts, especially your Spirit. Help me be open to this transforming gift.

Which of the fruits of the Spirit mentioned in Galatians 5 do you need most? Today ask God to produce that fruit in you by the power of God's Spirit.

■ ANSWERS TO PRAYER

Psalm 116: "I love the Lord, for he heard my voice; he heard my cry for mercy" (v. 1).

After much planning my mother and I were able to take a trip to Europe. For her it was the trip of a lifetime. She was especially looking forward to seeing the Alps in Switzerland. I wanted everything on the trip to be special for her. As we rode on the bus, I prayed that the weather would be clear so she would have an open view of the mountains. When we crossed into Switzerland, it was gray and overcast, the mountains hidden in dense fog. I continued to pray. The next morning the weather cleared, and for the next week we had sunshine and splendid Alpine views. I learned that the weather had been rainy for 25 days before we came. It cleared up the week we were there, and then the day we left it clouded up again.

Coincidence? Perhaps. One can never prove otherwise. But I have come to believe with William Temple, "When I pray, coincidences happen; when I don't, they don't." Martin Luther said, "Prayer is a powerful thing, for God has bound and tied himself to it. None can value how powerful prayer is, and what it is able to accomplish, except those who have learned by experience."

 Lord, I thank you for all the answers to prayer you have given me.

Recall some times when you have experienced answers to prayer. Share the memory with one person you trust.

■ FRIEND OF GOD

Exod. 33:7-11: "The Lord would speak to Moses face to face, as a man speaks with his friend" (v. 11).

One of the richest words in the English language is *friend*. It suggests intimacy, love, a close personal relationship. God wants to be for you more than an idea, a hypothesis, a doctrine. God wants to be your friend. God wants to talk with you as he talked to Moses, "face to face." Jesus said to those who believed in him, "I no longer call you servants . . . . Instead, I have called you friends" (John 15:15).

We know that a friendship requires communication—conversation, a phone call, a letter. By communicating we get to know one another. Marriage and family life also depend on people talking together and listening to one another. Prayer is our friendship with God. How can we know God unless we take time to talk with God—and to listen?

Through prayer you can come to know God, in the full biblical sense of that word. God will be your friend, as the beloved hymn declares:

> *What a friend we have in Jesus,*
> *All our sins and griefs to bear!*
> *What a privilege to carry*
> *Everything to God in prayer.*

 Lord of love, thank you for calling me your friend.

Think of one of your strongest friendships. What part does communication play in it? Apply this to your friendship with God.

■ BE RADIANT

Psalm 34: "Those who look to him are radiant; their faces are never covered with shame" (v. 5).

Have you ever noticed the special glow that people have who pray a great deal? Prayer does that to people. When Moses returned from the mountain after communicating with God for 40 days, his face shone (Exod. 34:29). It was when Jesus was praying that he was transfigured before his disciples, and "the appearance of his face changed, and his clothes became as bright as a flash of lightning" (Luke 9:29).

Dr. Alexis Carrel, M.D., wrote: "Prayer is not only worship; it is also an invisible emanation of man's worshipping spirit—the most powerful form of energy that one can generate. The influence of prayer on the human mind and body is as demonstrable as that of secreting glands. Its results can be measured in terms of increased physical buoyancy, greater intellectual vigor, moral stamina, and a deeper understanding of the realities underlying human relationships."

If you make a habit of sincere prayer, your life will be changed. You will be able to say, "I sought the Lord, and he answered me; he delivered me from all my fears" (v. 4).

 O God of light, brighten my life through your saving and transforming power.

Think of those you know who are people of prayer. How does prayer seem to affect them?

■ BE TRANSFORMED

Rom. 12:1-8: "Do not conform any longer to the pattern of this world, but be transformed by the renewing of your mind" (v. 2).

I like the way J. B. Phillips translates this verse: "Don't let the world around you squeeze you into its own mold but let God remold your minds from within, so that you may prove in practice that the plan of God for you is good, meets all his demands and moves toward the goal of true maturity." Peter said it this way: "Grow in the grace and knowledge of our Lord and Savior Jesus Christ" (2 Peter 3:18).

Prayer, including our listening to God's Word, is one of the ways by which God remolds our minds and moves us toward the goal of true maturity. When we pray, we are open to the transforming power of God. Indeed, the highest prayer is not "Give me," but, "Change me."

To come near to God is to change. He saves us from conformity to this passing world, and tunes us to the music of eternity.

Create in me a new heart, Lord,
That gladly I obey your Word.
Let what you will be my desire,
And with new life my soul inspire.

Make a list of some ways in which you would like to be "remolded." Pray about that today.

■ JESUS THE INTERCESSOR

Rom. 8:28-39:   "Christ Jesus, who died—more than
that, who was raised to life—is at the right hand of
God and is also interceding for us" (v. 34).

We turn now to the subject of intercession, to prayer
for others. An intercessor is literally a *go-between*, one
who bridges the gap between one person and another.
Jesus is the great go-between, who by his life and
death restored the relationship between God and
God's wandering children. And he continues this work
as part of his ministry as our great High Priest. In
Hebrews we read: "Because Jesus lives forever, he has
a permanent priesthood. Therefore he is able to save
completely those who come to God through him,
because he always lives to intercede for them" (Heb.
7:24-25).

Jesus is praying for you! Let that thought sink
deeply into your mind. We often ask a dear friend to
pray for us, but Jesus the Savior, who gave himself for
you, also now prays for you. He knows all your needs
and he stands as your go-between with God.

Jesus intercedes for us, and he is also the model for
our own intercession. In *The Believer's School of
Prayer* Andrew Murray wrote: "Christ, as Head, is
Intercessor in heaven; we, as members of His Body,
are partners with Him on earth."

 Blessed Jesus, I thank you that you are even
now praying for me. Fill me with your love that I
may be moved to pray for others.

**Read again through Rom. 8:28-39 and list all the
promises God makes to you there.**

■ FOR ALL THE SAINTS

Eph. 6:10-18: "And pray in the Spirit on all occasions with all kinds of prayers and requests. With this in mind, be alert and always keep on praying for all the saints" (v. 18).

As prayer partners with Jesus we have the privilege of serving as channels for God's blessings to others. Although intercession always remains something of a mystery, it seems there are some good things God will not or cannot do unless we pray. In *True Prayer* Kenneth Leech wrote: "Intercessory prayer is not a technique for changing God's mind, but it is a releasing of God's power through placing ourselves in a relationship of cooperation with God."

When we pray for others, we bring them into the flow of God's healing and blessing power. We do not always know what these people need. It is not that we are trying to impose our will on God or on them, but we gently lift them into God's presence, asking simply that God's highest good may come to them.

We can never *prove* that intercession "works." But we have God's command and the example of Jesus to motivate us to "be alert and always keep on praying for all the saints."

 O Spirit of prayer, I don't know how intercession works, but I will do it because you urge me to do it.

Today think of three people who especially need your prayers. Picture yourself bringing them to Jesus and asking him to bless them.

■ THOSE NEAREST TO US

Eph. 1:15-20: "I have not stopped giving thanks for you, remembering you in my prayers" (v. 16).

Love and intercession belong together. If you love people and if you believe in God, you will pray for them. Pray for them, and you will love them more.

It is natural that we begin with those nearest to us, those with whom we live, the friends who are dearest to us, the groups to which we belong. For these we should pray regularly and often. It need not be a long prayer, but every time we think of them, we can pray: "Lord, bless. . . ." "Lord, may your will be done. . . ."

Frank Laubach wrote: "Prayer is powerful, but it is not the power of a sledge hammer that crushes with one blow. It is the power of sun rays and raindrops which bless, because there are so many of them. Instead of a minute a day, we Christians must learn to flash hundreds of instantaneous prayers at people near and far, knowing that many prayers will show no visible results, but that at least some of them will hit near their mark. When you fill a swamp with stones, a hundred loads may disappear under the water before a stone appears on the surface, but all of them are necessary."

 Lord, fill me with love for those nearest to me and let that love spill over into prayer.

Choose five people you especially love. Each time you think of them today, thank God for them and offer a brief prayer on their behalf.

58

■ THE DEBT OF INTERCESSION

1 Sam. 12:19-25: "As for me, far be it from me that I should sin against the Lord by failing to pray for you" (v. 23).

An old farmer is said to have prayed: "God bless me and my wife, my son John and his wife, us four and no more. Amen." Our prayers may begin with those closest to us, but they should not end there. Others need our prayers, and we need to pray for them. The Bible does not present intercession as optional. In his farewell speech to Israel, Samuel went so far as to say that failing to pray for others is a sin.

But there are so many who need our prayers, and we have only limited time in which to pray. What are we to do?

You probably will want to pray every day for those special few that God lays on your heart or those who need your prayer most. For the rest you may need some system. One way is to spread your prayer concerns over the days of the week. For example, on Sunday pray for your local congregation and its leadership; Monday—for your work, the work of others, and for the unemployed; Tuesday—for the sick and handicapped and those in healing work; Wednesday—for world affairs and those in government; Thursday—for your extended family; Friday—for students, teachers, and schools; and Saturday—for friends.

With a plan like this we will always be ready to pay the debt of intercession we owe.

 O Holy Spirit, reveal to me those for whom I should pray.

For one week try the plan of intercession suggested here.

■ HOLDING UP THE PROPHET'S HANDS

Exod. 17:8-13: "When Moses' hands grew tired, they took a stone and put it under him and he sat on it. Aaron and Hur held his hands up—one on one side, and one on the other—so that his hands remained steady until sunset" (v. 12).

It must have looked as if the men fighting in the valley were doing the real work, but Israel's fortune depended on Moses' arms raised in blessing. The outcome was not determined only by the fighters in the battle, but also by the intercessors on the mountain and by those who held up the tired arms of the prophet.

Like Moses, your pastor gets weary. He or she needs your prayers. You can undergird your pastor's preaching and teaching and counseling and evangelizing by your intercession. This is work for all Christians—including elderly people and those who are home-bound. An old hymn says it well:

> *If you cannot be a watchman*
> *Standing high on Zion's wall.*
> *Pointing out the path to heaven.*
> *Off'ring life and peace to all.*
> *With your prayers and with your bounties*
> *You can do what God demands:*
> *You can be like faithful Aaron,*
> *Holding up the prophet's hands.*

I thank you, Holy Spirit, for my pastor. I want to be faithful in holding up the prophet's hands.

Tell your pastor you are praying for him or her. Ask if there are any special needs for which you should pray.

■ PRAYER FOR GOVERNMENT

1 Tim. 2:1-6: "I urge, then, first of all, that requests, prayers, intercession and thanksgiving be made for everyone—for kings and all those in authority, that we may live peaceful and quiet lives in all godliness and holiness" (vv. 1-2).

If we spent as much time praying for politicians as we do complaining about them, think of the difference it would make! The early Christians had as much a right to complain as we—even more, for they had a government that persecuted them for their faith. Yet the early Christian leader Polycarp said, "We pray for all saints, for kings and rulers, for our persecutors and for the enemies of the cross."

It is well to make our praying specific, to have a list of those national, state, and local officials for whom we pray, asking that God would give them the wisdom, compassion, and integrity they need. Perhaps in our time of prayer God will give us an idea of something we need to do, like writing a letter or taking some other action. Be alert to any nudges in that direction.

While we pray for our own government, we think of other world leaders and pray for God's influence on them. We remember all who are working for peace in the world. We never know how much events are dependent on the hidden work of God's intercessors.

 Heavenly King, bless all rulers everywhere and give them your heart of love and justice.

Today make a list of those in government for whom you will pray at least once a week.

■ FOR THOSE IN PRISON

Acts 12:1-17: "So Peter was kept in prison, but the church was earnestly praying to God for him" (v. 5).

Imagine what it must have been like for the servant girl named Rhoda. Perhaps she was among those who prayed for Peter, and perhaps she wasn't sure anything would happen. So when she answered the knock on the door, she was so amazed that she left poor Peter standing there—with a smile on his face, I imagine.

Peter was what we today call a prisoner of conscience. There are thousands like him throughout the world. Organizations like Amnesty International remember these people and try to work for their release. Through an organization like that and with our prayers we can help those who are imprisoned for their faith or their political convictions.

Criminals also need our prayers, as they so often live with no hope in surroundings that are demeaning, frightening, and corrupting. Others are imprisoned by alcohol or drugs, compulsions or fears. They need our prayers that God's releasing power can enter their lives. Then they too will sing, "God's Son has made me free."

 O Lord, bless all those who are in any way imprisoned.

Think of someone you know who is "imprisoned" in some way. Pray for that person today.

■ PRAYING FOR THE SICK

James 5:13-20:   "Therefore confess your sins to
each other and pray for each other so that you may
be healed. The prayer of a righteous man is
powerful and effective" (v. 16).

Prayer for healing was a vital part of the ministry of
the early church. Its renewal in our time coincides
with our interest in holistic medicine, which
recognizes that sickness often is a sign of deep spiritual
need.

James here suggests that the elders of a church pray
for a sick person. Sometimes we may be present to
pray with the sick person. At other times we may
simply by prayer carry our friends into the presence of
Jesus, asking for healing in whatever form God
chooses to send.

God heals through the cooperation of doctors,
nurses, and therapists. God heals in ways we
understand so little that we call them miracles. The
healing may be spiritual, strengthening us to endure
suffering with patience. Sometimes God restores
wholeness only beyond death.

We do not dictate how God is to heal. We simply
bring our sick before God, trusting in God's love and
promise of healing.

 Lord, you have promised that prayer is
powerful and effective. I trust in your ability to
heal.

**Think today of those you know who are sick in mind
or body. In your imagination bring them one by one
to Jesus and place their hands in his.**

■ HARVEST WORKERS

Matt. 9:35-38: "The harvest is plentiful but the workers are few. Ask the Lord of the harvest, therefore, to send out workers into his harvest field" (vv. 37-38).

Jesus was filled with compassion for the multitudes who had no spiritual guides. Where would the workers come from? Jesus' answer: through prayer.

Missionaries are still needed—not only to bring the news of God's love to those who have never heard, but also to help feed the hungry, provide medical care, teach needed skills, bring agricultural aid. We cannot all go overseas to do the work, but we can all pray that the Spirit will move some to go and still others to provide financial resources. And then we can support missionaries, native workers, and support staff with our prayers.

In *The Believer's School of Prayer* Andrew Murray wrote, "Christ means to teach us that however large the field may be, and however few the laborers, prayer is the best, the sure, the only means for supplying the need."

 Lord of the harvest, you know the needs of the world, and you know those who could help meet those needs. May your Spirit speak to those you would send into your harvest. Keep us faithful who support them at home.

Does your congregation support a missionary? Make that individual or family the special object of your prayers. Write a letter to let them know you are praying for them.

■ FOR THE OPPRESSED

Psalm 69:   "The Lord hears the needy and does not despise his captive people" (v. 33).

Many are bothered by these "imprecatory" or "cursing" psalms, because they seem so far from the spirit of Jesus. Some are ready to delete these from the Bible as unworthy of Christians, but before we do that, we should look again at their value.

First of all, they underscore the importance of honesty in prayer. There is no phoniness in these prayers, no attempt to deny feelings of revenge or anger. These psalms show us how victims really feel, and how oppressed people bring even their most hateful feelings into God's presence

What has helped me most is the suggestion that though we may feel no need to pray these prayers for ourselves, we can pray them on behalf of all the victims of oppression, all those who have been crushed by the rich and powerful of the world, all those whose only hope is in God.

 O God, a psalm like this takes me deep into the pain of the world. Let me not shrink from the pain, but make this psalm my prayer for the oppressed.

Think of the oppressed peasant in South America, the starving poor in Africa, the victims of racial prejudice. Pray Psalm 69 for them.

■ EVEN FOR ENEMIES

Luke 6:27-36: "Love your enemies, do good to those who hate you, bless those who curse you, pray for those who mistreat you" (vv. 27-28).

While the Psalms contain prayers *against* the enemy, Jesus calls on us to pray *for* our enemies. And he incarnated this prayer on the cross when he prayed, "Father, forgive them, for they do not know what they are doing" (Luke 23:34).

Our prayer for those who have mistreated us not only blesses them but is a sure way of dissolving our own hatred and resentment. Bonhoeffer said it so well in *Life Together:* "A Christian fellowship lives and exists by the intercession of its members for one another, or it collapses. I can no longer condemn or hate a brother for whom I pray, no matter how much trouble he causes me. His face, that hitherto may have been strange and intolerable to me, is transformed in intercession into the countenance of a brother for whom Christ died, the face of a forgiven sinner. . . . There is no dislike, no personal tension, no estrangement that cannot be overcome by intercession as far as our side of it is concerned. Intercessory prayer is the purifying bath into which that individual and the fellowship must enter every day."

 Lord Jesus, may your prayer for your enemies move me to pray for mine.

Think of one or two people for whom you harbor bad feelings. Pray for them today.

■ THE COSTLINESS OF INTERCESSION

Exod. 32:31-34:   "But now, please forgive their
sin—but if not, then blot me out of the book you
have written" (v. 32).

Moses was one of the great intercessors of the Old
Testament. While he was on Mount Sinai, the people
of Israel lost faith in God and worshiped the golden
calf. Although Moses was furious at them, he
interceded on their behalf, asking God to forgive
them. He even put his own soul on the line, willing to
have his name blotted out of the book of life.

Intercession is like that. It is not a glib substitute for
true concern—"Well, I'll pray about it." When we
intercede for another, we should also be willing to do
what we can for that person. Praying for the world's
hungry may mean reaching for my checkbook. Praying
for an enemy may mean offering an apology. Praying
for my pastor may mean volunteering to help.

Intercession is cooperation with God. It may begin
with words, but it often requires our actions.

 Lord, I don't want prayer to be a way of
avoiding service. If there's something I should
do, show me and give me the strength and will
to do it.

**Think of those for whom you have been praying. If
you feel led by God, take some action that seems
right and possible for you.**

■ PRAY FOR ME

2 Thess. 3:1-5: "Finally, brothers, pray for us . . ."
(v. 1).

Paul depended on the prayers of his friends. To the
Corinthians he wrote: "On him we have set our hope
that he will continue to deliver us, as you help us by
your prayers. Then many will give thanks on our
behalf for the gracious favor granted us in answer to
the prayers of many" (2 Cor. 1:10-11).

I am writing these words at a retreat house in
southern Minnesota. Before I came, I asked a number
of friends to pray for me, and now as I work I feel
buoyed up and strengthened by the knowledge that
they are helping with their prayers.

Intercession is a two-way street. We pray for others,
but it is also right to ask other people to pray for us. I
have friends who have offered to pray for me weekly
or even daily. I often send them specific requests, and
I let them know when God has answered this prayer.

I consider this one of my greatest blessings that I
have friends who pray for me. I pray that you, too,
will be so blessed.

 Lord of love, thank you for those who pray for
me. Give me courage to ask others for their
prayers.

**Think of one friend who prays. In a letter or
conversation ask that person to pray for you and
give the friend a special list of concerns.**

■ FREELY BY HIS GRACE

Rom. 3:21-31: "For all have sinned and fall short of the glory of God and are justified freely by his grace through the redemption that came by Christ Jesus" (vv. 23-24).

We have been looking at the kinds of prayer called *supplication*—the prayer of asking, both for ourselves and for others. Perhaps that is the kind of prayer we think of first, but it is not the only kind. Let us now look at the prayer of *confession*.

We are flawed people. We use all sorts of words to describe that flaw: failure, brokenness, alienation, phoniness, selfishness. The Bible calls it *sin*. It is part of the human condition, a sign of separation from God.

God has done something about sin. God became one with us in the person of his Son, Jesus Christ. Through Christ's life, death, and resurrection, in ways we cannot comprehend, we are made right with God. We do not have to redeem ourselves. The redemption has been accomplished through Jesus. This is the ground of our faith. With this hope we sinners dare to pray.

 Lord Jesus, I don't fully understand how your death overcame the power of sin, but I believe it.

Personalize the promise of Rom. 3:23-24 by saying: "I have sinned and fall short of the glory of God, but I have been justified freely by God's grace through the redemption that came by Christ Jesus."

■ THE NEED FOR FORGIVENESS

Luke 18:9-14:   "Everyone who exalts himself will be humbled, and he who humbles himself will be exalted" (v. 14).

When friends or family members disagree, the tension often grows worse and worse until someone says, "I'm sorry." Then reconciliation can begin.

The Pharisee and the tax collector typify two different attitudes toward prayer. The Pharisee comes offering God his own supposed goodness, his spiritual accomplishments. The tax collector comes as a beggar, with empty hands, conscious only of his need for forgiveness. He alone found the way to God.

In *Beginning to Pray* Anthony Bloom wrote, "What we must start with, if we wish to pray, is the certainty that we are sinners in need of salvation, that we are cut off from God and that we cannot live without him and that all we can offer God is our desperate longing to be made such that God will receive us, receive us in repentance, receive us with mercy and with love."

 God, have mercy on me a sinner.

Reflect on this statement: "Nothing that we are sorry for separates us from God."

70

■ CONFESSION

Psalm 32: "Then I acknowledged my sin to you and did not cover up my iniquity. I said, 'I will confess my transgressions to the Lord'—and you forgave the guilt of my sin" (v. 5).

Confession begins with self-examination, which is not morbid introspection or self-condemnation, but an honest, fearless look at one's self. We begin by asking the Holy Spirit to show us our faults and what lies behind them.

Confession is best done daily, perhaps in conjunction with our evening prayer. But we need not wait that long. Someone has urged us to "keep short accounts with God." At any moment that we are aware of sin, we can stop and say "I have sinned. Lord, forgive."

In one sense confession is painful, because it forces us to face our own limitations and brokenness. Yet in another way, it is a great relief. As the psalmist puts it, "When I kept silent, my bones wasted away . . . your hand was heavy upon me . . . my strength was sapped." Confession lances the festering sins within, opening the wound for Christ to heal.

"If you, O Lord, kept a record of sins, O Lord, who could stand? But with you there is forgiveness" (Ps. 130:3-4).

Use 1 Corinthians 13 as the basis for self-examination, and confess your sins against love.

■ RECEIVING FORGIVENESS

Isa. 43:25: "I, even I, am he who blots out your transgressions, for my own sake, and remembers your sin no more."

In his *Letters* C. S Lewis said, "A sin once repented and forgiven is gone, annihilated, burnt up in the fire of Divine Love, white as snow. There is no harm in continuing to 'bewail' it, i.e., to express one's sorrow, but not to ask for pardon, for that you have already."

By faith we know that God has forgiven our sins, yet we may not always feel forgiven. Feelings of "If only. . ." remain to haunt us. Sometimes we have to talk ourselves back into accepting God's forgiveness. If God forgives us, we must forgive ourselves. Otherwise we set ourselves up as a judge higher than God.

It may help us to remember the experience of Christian in *Pilgrim's Progress:* "So I saw in my dream, that just as Christian came up with the cross, his burden loosed from off his shoulders, and fell from off his back, and began to tumble; and so continued to do, till it came to the mouth of the sepulchre, where it fell in, *and I saw it no more."*

 Lord of mercy, since you forgive my sins, help me to let them go too.

It may help you to take some symbolic action in order to receive God's forgiveness. If there is a sin that especially bothers you, write it on a piece of paper, claim God's forgiveness, and then burn the paper. Or confess to your pastor or a trusted friend.

■ SET FREE

1 John 1:5-10: "If we confess our sins, he is faithful and just and will forgive us our sins and purify us from all unrighteousness" (v. 9).

God not only wants to forgive our sins; God wants to take them away, to set us free from them. It can be easy to fall into the trap of wanting to be free of the penalty of the sin, but not the sin itself. Dietrich Bonhoeffer called this "cheap grace."

Already in the early church this was a problem, so Paul had to write: "What shall we say, then? Shall we go on sinning so that grace may increase? By no means! We died to sin; how can we live in it any longer?" (Rom. 6:1-2).

In Christ we are a new creation. The Holy Spirit is ever at work to transform us, to make us more and more like Jesus. This process of purifying or cleansing usually takes time. Habits that have been formed over many years are usually not eradicated in a moment. In the daily process of dying to sin and being reborn to new life, we hold on to God's promise: "If we confess our sins, he is faithful and just and will forgive us our sins and purify us from all unrighteousness."

 "Create in me a pure heart, O God, and renew a steadfast spirit within me" (Ps. 51:10).

Is there a sin you have been hanging on to? Today ask God not only to forgive it, but to purify you from it.

■ PRAISE THE LORD

Psalm 150: "Let everything that has breath praise the Lord" (v. 6).

We have looked at prayers of petition, intercession, and confession. Another aspect of prayer is praise and thanksgiving. Praise expresses to God what you believe about him: "Lord God, you made me, you know me, you are in me, sustaining me, guiding me, correcting me." Such a prayer of praise gives glory to God and builds our faith by reminding us of the great truths of life.

It is good to begin a time of prayer with an act of praise. This moves our thoughts away from our own confusion and trouble, and lifts them to God. The essence of praise is in the words, "Lift up your hearts."

Praise may not come as naturally as our cries for help, but we have a treasury of words we can use for praise. The Psalms are an especially rich source, as are many hymns. We can sing some of the great hymns of praise—by ourselves or with others. Or, we can speak them silently and slowly, pondering the meaning of the words and what they teach us about God.

 "O Lord, open my lips, and my mouth will declare your praise" (Ps. 51:15).

Today find a psalm and a hymn verse you can use to express your praise of God.

■ CONTINUAL PRAISE

Psalm 71:1-8: "My mouth is filled with your praise, declaring your splendor all day long" (v. 8).

Just as we use "dart" or "flash" prayers of petition, we can punctuate our days with short bursts of praise. As we become sensitive to the times God meets us with an insight, a flash of guidance, an answer to prayer, strength for a task, a wave of love that overcomes resentment, an experience of beauty, we turn to God in praise. You may want to use a brief phrase like one of these:

"Glory to you, O Lord."

"I love you, O Lord, my strength" (Ps. 18:1).

"Thank you, Lord!"

"To you, O Lord, I lift up my soul" (Ps. 25:1).

"My God and my all!"

"I will praise you as long as I live" (Ps. 63:4).

Such frequent acts of praise lift our hearts and minds to God and refresh our spirits.

 "I will exalt you, my God the King; I will praise your name for ever and ever. Every day I will praise you and extol your name for ever and ever" (Ps. 145:1-2).

Choose one brief prayer of praise, memorize it, and use it often today.

■ THROUGHOUT ALL THE WORLD

Psalm 113: "From the rising of the sun to the place where it sets the name of the Lord is to be praised" (v. 3).

Have you ever experienced the thrill of singing hymns of praise in a large church or a special gathering? Although you may not feel it as strongly, you are joined with all the faithful when you praise God in the solitude of your own room. Your voice is being added to the great chorus of praise that rises to God from the entire planet. A favorite evening hymn pictures this ongoing adoration.

> *We thank you that your church unsleeping*
> *While earth rolls onward into light.*
> *Through all the world its watch is keeping,*
> *And never rests by day or night.*
>
> *As to each continent and island*
> *The dawn leads on another day.*
> *The voice of prayer is never silent,*
> *Nor dies the strain of praise away.*
>
> *The sun, here having set, is waking*
> *Your children under western skies,*
> *And hour by hour, as day is breaking,*
> *Fresh hymns of thankful praise arise.*

 I thank you, Father of all, that I can praise you together with the whole people of God.

Take time to ponder the thought that all through the world, 24 hours a day, God's people are praying and praising.

■ FORGET NOT

Psalm 103: "Praise the Lord, O my soul, and forget not all his benefits" (v. 2).

He was an old man, terribly crippled with arthritis. I had to help him on with his coat and then lift him into the car. When we came to the restaurant, it took him a long time to shuffle to the table. I had to open the package of sugar for his coffee. Before we ate, he bowed his head and prayed, "Bless the Lord, O my soul, and forget not all his benefits." He had learned the strength that comes from a thankful heart—and he taught me a lesson I will not forget.

Especially when we get swamped by the worries and troubles of life, we need to stop and remember God's benefits. There is wisdom in the old song: "Count your many blessings, name them one by one." I have found that when I feel depressed or self-pitying, I am almost immediately lifted up if I take time to thank God specifically for my blessings, naming them one by one, even in writing.

The German dramatist Lessing wrote: "A single thankful thought towards heaven is the most perfect of all prayers."

 Lord, you have given me so much. Give me one more thing—a grateful heart.

Take paper and pencil and list all the things for which you have to be thankful. Keep the list and add to it from time to time.

■ GROWING IN GRATITUDE

Luke 17:11-19: "Was no one found to return and give praise to God except this foreigner?" (v. 18).

For four years I lived with my family in a small town in a remote corner of Madagascar. While we lived much better than almost all the local people, we did miss some things which we had taken for granted in the United States. Now, even five years after our return, I find I am still grateful for simple things like fresh milk, an abundance of water, a piece of cheese, or a new book.

Just because we have so much, we often forget to express our gratitude. Like the nine lepers, we go on our way with no thought of giving thanks. In *Growth in Prayer* Constance Garrett explains how to develop a habit of gratitude: "Until we stop and realize those things for which we can be thankful, we are not thankful. As we give expression to our thanks, the impression is deepened. And the more conscious we are of things to be thankful for, the more we enjoy them and the better we use them."

 Giver of all good things, help me to develop the habit of gratitude.

Create a litany of thanksgiving. Begin each phrase with: "For . . . ." Add the words, "I give you thanks, O Lord."

■ THANKS FOR EVERYTHING

Eph. 5:15-20: "Speak to one another with psalms, hymns, and spiritual songs . . . . always giving thanks to God the Father for everything, in the name of our Lord Jesus Christ" (vv. 19-20).

Thanksgiving is not only a debt we owe to God; it also transforms us. It strengthens our love for God and makes us happier and more positive people. Therefore the more we can thank God, the better.

The apostle Paul, no stranger to persecution and hardship, spoke of "giving thanks for everything" and urged us to "give thanks in all circumstances" (1 Thess. 5:18). Is this really possible? How can we thank God for illness, unemployment, or failure?

I don't believe that God deliberately sends us evil, but in governing the world, he does not grant us immunity from pain or death. I do believe that God permits nothing to come to us that he cannot use for our spiritual growth and his glory.

E. Stanley Jones said, "I find myself thanking God for everything, for everything furthers you deeper into God if you let it."

 Lord, teach me to be grateful for all of life, knowing you are there working for my good.

Can you identify a bad situation in your life out of which God brought some good? Thank him for it now.

■ THE JESUS PRAYER

Matt. 9:27-36: "As Jesus went on from there, two blind men followed him calling out, 'Have mercy on us, Son of David' " (v. 27).

In a famous Russian classic on prayer, *The Way of a Pilgrim,* a peasant hears the words from Thessalonians, "Pray without ceasing." He wonders how to do this until a holy man teaches him the Jesus Prayer, "Lord Jesus Christ, Son of God, have mercy on me, a sinner." He learns to pray it as the background for his whole life.

Since then many people have found it a helpful prayer. It can be prayed quietly in time with one's breathing—breathing in on "Lord Jesus Christ," out on "Son of God," in on "have mercy on me," and out on "a sinner."

One friend prays the Jesus prayer while jogging. I often pray it when I'm too tired to pray anything else. Sometimes I use a shortened form, "Lord Jesus Christ, have mercy on me."

In certain ways it is a perfect prayer. It is brief. It focuses our thoughts on Jesus and who he is for us. It recognizes our dependence on him. It asks for his forgiveness and his help for all our needs.

 Spirit of life and power, thank you for this ancient prayer. Teach me what it can mean for my life.

Today set aside a few minutes in which to pray the Jesus Prayer.

■ PRACTICING THE PRESENCE

Psalm 16: "You have made known to me the path of life; you will fill me with joy in your presence, with eternal pleasures at your right hand" (v. 11).

God is always with us. We can't escape God, even if we want to. Yet often we are not aware of God's presence. In times of despair or dryness, we may feel as if God is absent. We can't make that sense of presence happen. It is always a gift. Yet with practice, it is possible to develop a habit of mind in which we are more aware of God's nearness.

In the 16th century, a lay brother discovered how to be aware of God in the midst of his daily duties. He called this "practicing the presence of God." Brother Lawrence wrote: "God lays no great burden upon us; a little remembrance of him from time to time, a little adoration, sometimes to pray for his grace, sometimes to offer him your sorrows, and sometimes to return him thanks for the benefits he has given you, and still gives you in the midst of your troubles. He asks you to console yourself with him the oftenest you can. Lift up your heart to him even at your meals and when you are in company; the least little remembrance will always be acceptable to him. You need not cry very loud; he is nearer to us than we think."

 Lord, I believe that I am always in your presence. Make me be more aware of your presence day by day.

Today try to think of God at least once every hour, and offer a brief prayer.

■ THE PRAYER OF AFFIRMATION

Psalm 23: "Surely goodness and love will follow me all the days of my life, and I will dwell in the house of the Lord forever" (v. 6).

Bonhoeffer called the Psalms the "prayerbook of the Bible." Of all the prayers in this collection none is so well-loved as this Shepherd Psalm. Note that this prayer does not ask anything of God. It does not ask God to be my shepherd; it affirms that God is. It does not ask for guidance; it assumes guidance is being given. It is a prayer of affirmation, a statement of what we believe about God and his care for us.

This type of prayer is useful in overcoming doubt and giving a positive tone to the day. Many Bible verses, like these in Psalm 23 can be used as affirmations. Or we can create our own statements of faith, like, "Lord, I know you're with me always," "God, I believe that you love me," "Heavenly Father, I rest in your care."

We can say a faith statement like this quietly and confidently, perhaps repeating it over and over. If we have it memorized, we can do this just before falling asleep. The words will then sink deep into our unconscious mind, creating deep peace and confidence.

 Faithful Lord, help me focus not on my problems, but on your promises.

Begin a collection of short affirmations you can use throughout your day.

■ HOW NOT TO PRAY

Matt. 6:5-8: "And when you pray, do not keep on babbling like pagans, for they think they will be heard because of their many words" (v. 7).

Having looked at various ways to pray, let us turn to some of the difficulties we have in prayer.

In the Sermon on the Mount, Jesus gives two warnings about prayer. First, we are not to pray in order to impress others with our religiousness. Our prayers are not to be directed to other people, but to God. This temptation to show off with our prayers may be a problem for some, but I think more of us have the opposite problem: we need greater boldness to pray before others, not to draw attention to ourselves, but to witness to our faith.

Second, we do not need to use many words in order to inform God or to break down his resistance. God knows our needs, and we pray not for his benefit, but for our own, that we may know the peace that comes from bringing our needs before God. For this a brief prayer is sufficient. Luther even said, "The fewer the words, the better the prayer."

 Lord, help me to pray with pure motive and few words.

How can you apply these words of Jesus to your prayer life?

■ WORDS WITHOUT THOUGHTS

Isa. 29:13-24: "These people come near to me with their mouth and honor me with their lips, but their hearts are far from me" (v. 13).

My words fly up, my thoughts remain below. Words without thoughts never to heaven go." So prayed the king in Shakespeare's *Hamlet*. Sometimes that is our experience too. In public prayer or in solitude, using formulated prayers or spontaneous ones, we draw near to God with our lips, while our hearts remain distant.

In dealing with this problem we have to strike a balance. On the one hand, a mindless rattling off of words is not prayer, at least not prayer as God intends. We should never settle for that.

On the other hand, we have to accept our human limitations. Already as a young boy I struggled with trying to pray the Lord's Prayer while concentrating on the meaning of all the words. I'm not sure I ever succeeded. If we set an impossible standard for ourselves, frustrations may cause us to quit praying altogether.

Especially in times of weariness or distraction we have to pray the best we can and count on God to accept that. If we can't pray, we can at least *say* our prayers. And that is not to be despised.

 O God of mercy, forgive me when I pray empty words. Enable me to pray the best I can.

When do you find it hardest to pray with meaning? What could you do about that?

■ WRONG MOTIVES

James 4:1-10: "You do not have, because you do not ask God. When you ask, you do not receive, because you ask with wrong motives, that you may spend what you get on your pleasures" (vv. 2-3).

James identifies two reasons why we do not experience all the blessings of answered prayer.

First, "You do not have, because you do not ask God." These seem to me to be some of the saddest words in the Bible, but I know how true they are. I sometimes catch myself wrestling with a problem for days until I think, "But I haven't prayed about that yet." We forget to pray, or we think we don't have time, or we doubt that it will do any good. And we are the losers for it.

Even when we do pray, says James, we sometimes do not receive what we ask for because we ask with wrong motives. We ask, not as servants, but as selfish pleasure-seekers. Think of the harm that would come if God answered every prayer that was motivated by greed or revenge or lust. Would you want to live in such a world? Prayer is not automatic magic. Thank God, it isn't. We come making a request of the King, knowing God may choose to say no—but trusting that even God's refusals are for our good.

 Holy Spirit, purify my motives, so that I ask only according to your will.

Is there something you have been praying about which God seems to ignore? Ask God to show you whether there is something wrong with your motivation.

■ SUFFICIENT GRACE

2 Cor. 12:1-10: "Three times I pleaded with the Lord to take it away from me. But he said to me, 'My grace is sufficient for you, for my power is made perfect in weakness' " (v. 8).

What was Paul's thorn in the flesh? We simply don't know. Whatever it was, it seems to have been both painful and persistent. Three times this great man of faith asked that this thorn be removed, and God's only answer was, "My grace is sufficient for you."

Leslie Weatherhead wrote in *A Private House of Prayer*, "The man who has found God has not insured himself against calamity. But he has found One who will show him how to turn calamity into triumph. He will not escape the thorns of life. But he will wear them as a crown."

When sickness or tragedy strikes, we may cry out, "Why does God allow this to happen?" "Why doesn't he do something?" The Bible gives no final, intellectual answer to questions like these. It redirects us to ask a different question: "What can I do about this?" It directs us to look to God for strength. Even in our weakness God's grace and power can come through.

 Mighty Lord, may your power be made perfect in my weakness.

What does the phrase "My power is made perfect in your weakness" mean in your life?

■ DISTRACTIONS

Phil. 4:7: "And the peace of God, which transcends all understanding, will guard your hearts and your minds in Christ Jesus."

I come into solitude and silence to pray. The room may be quiet, but inside my head is blooming confusion. I begin to pray, and I think of something I need to do this afternoon, or I remember a friend who asked me to call, or I think of something I heard on the six o'clock news. Such distractions come to all who pray. How do we best handle them?

First of all, don't try to fight them. Wrestling with them only strengthens the distraction and wearies you. I've found two alternatives. One is just to notice these things and then look beyond them and continue praying. Just let the distractions slip by.

If the distractions are more persistent, I quickly incorporate them into my prayer. In a few sentences I ask for God's help, blessing, or forgiveness, and then go on.

In *Prayer in Other Words* Dom Hubert von Zeller gives this advice: "Try not to let your prayer go round and round in circles with you as the center of it. Your prayer is meant to go out from you towards God. The more you try to love him and forget about yourself the better."

 Lord, calm my restless thoughts. Let your peace guard my heart and mind.

The next time you experience distractions in prayer, try one of the methods above for handling them.

■ DRYNESS IN PRAYER

Psalm 63: "O God, you are my God, earnestly I seek you; my soul thirsts for you, my body longs for you, in a dry and weary land where there is no water" (v. 1).

Even the greatest saints report days of dryness when prayer seems unreal, boring, useless. Then we are tempted to give up on prayer, but that is just the time when we must continue. The famous preacher C. H. Spurgeon said, "We should pray when we are in a praying mood; for it would be sinful to neglect so fair an opportunity. We should pray when we are not in a proper mood; for it would be dangerous to remain in so unhealthy a condition."

What can help us keep praying in times of dryness? You might try changing the time at which you pray or the place. A book of written prayers may give you the words you need. It may be time to pray with another person.

Whatever we do, we should continue in quiet persistence, in spite of our feelings, looking forward to the time when rain comes in the desert of our soul and we are again able to say, "My soul will be satisfied as with the richest of foods; with singing lips my mouth will praise you" (v. 5).

 O God, keep me faithful to prayer, even in a dry and weary land.

Find a book of prayers you could use to help you pray in times of dryness.

■ PRAYER FOR WISDOM

James 1:2-8: "If any of you lacks wisdom, he should ask God, who gives generously to all without finding fault, and it will be given to him" (v. 5).

After I've driven around and around for over 20 minutes, getting more and more lost, my wife gets that certain look on her face and says, "Why don't you just stop and ask someone?"

The answer, of course, is that I want to do it myself. I don't want to look stupid, so I waste time and gas muddling around by myself. It's a lesson I'm trying to learn for all of life: "Why don't you just stop and ask someone?"

According to James, God does not find fault with us when we need wisdom, an answer to the practical realities of life. God gives generously. The only condition laid down is that we believe that the wisdom will come to us, through one of God's many channels: God's Word, friends and counselors, books, our own thoughts and desires, and sometimes ways we don't expect.

Once we've asked for wisdom, we should seek it in the best places we know, and then trust that when God's answer comes, we will recognize it for what it is.

 Lord of all wisdom, teach me what I need to know.

In what area of life do you feel the greatest need for wisdom? Ask God to provide it. Take one concrete step to seek that wisdom.

■ THE DESIRES OF YOUR HEART

Psalm 37:1-9: "Delight yourself in the Lord and he will give you the desires of your heart" (v. 4).

Some people are convinced that if they want something, it must not be God's will for them, that somehow it is wrong for them to have any desires of their own. In *The Teaching of Jesus on Prayer* Lewis Maclachlan counters that notion: "Our desires are a very important factor in making us what we are, and if bad desires can be our ruin, good desires can be our salvation. Instead of trying to quench desire, we should purify it and exalt it, and there is no better way of doing so than to make our requests known unto God."

Note that this verse does not promise we can have anything we want. There is a condition: "delight yourself in the Lord." You can't delight yourself in the Lord and desire your neighbor's spouse. You can't be in close relationship with God and ask out of selfishness or greed.

What God promises to give are the desires of your heart—not just momentary whims or desires fostered by our society, but the longings that come from the depths of the person God wants you to be.

 Lord, teach me to delight in you; then I can be sure you will give me the deepest desires of my heart.

What are the desires of your heart? Write them down and focus your prayers on them.

■ IF I HAD CHERISHED SIN

Psalm 66: "If I had cherished sin in my heart, the Lord would not have listened" (v. 18).

These are uncomfortable words, but words we need to hear. If we cherish sin, if we fondle it, hang on to it, justify it, God will not listen to our prayers. Sin always erects a barrier between us and another person, between us and our best selves, between us and God. The barrier can be removed by confession and forgiveness.

Forgiveness is a free gift, but repentance is costly. It involves admitting our wrong and being willing to be put right. George Macdonald warned, "No man is condemned for anything he has done: he is condemned for continuing to do wrong. He is condemned for not coming out of the darkness, for not coming to the light."

God, who shows us our sin, also wants to take that sin away. When that happens, we are able to say, "Praise be to God, who has not rejected my prayer or withheld his love from me!" (Ps. 66:20).

 O Lord of mercy and love, I realize that my sin creates a barrier between us. I'm asking you to remove that barrier.

Ponder the thought: "Forgiveness is free, but repentance is costly."

■ REQUEST DENIED

Mark 10:35-45: " 'You don't know what you are asking,' Jesus said. 'Can you drink the cup I drink or be baptized with the baptism I am baptized with?' " (v. 38).

James and John came with their impudent request—almost a demand—"We want you to do for us whatever we ask." Jesus allowed them to put forth their petition, but he did not grant their request.

We shouldn't be too hard on James and John. At least they came to Jesus, and with expectation. What they wanted wasn't so bad, but there were some problems. They were acting out of selfish ambition, and they did not realize the price involved—the cup or baptism of suffering that they would have to share with Jesus.

Jesus could not honor their prayer and be true to himself or his kingdom. To grant their request would have been to contradict the servant role to which he was calling them. So Jesus had to say, "You don't know what you're asking."

We too can bring any petition to Jesus, trusting him to correct our erring requests and point us back to his truth.

 Loving Lord, forgive my foolish prayers. I trust you to grant me something that is even better for me.

What does this story teach you about the kind of requests Jesus must deny?

■ NO THRILL EVER LASTS

Luke 9:28-36: "As the men were leaving Jesus, Peter said to him, 'Master, it is good for us to be here. Let us put up three shelters—one for you, one for Moses and one for Elijah.' (He did not know what he was saying.)" (v. 33).

It is good for us, too, to have a mountaintop experience now and then. Most of us can remember times when God's presence seemed especially real, perhaps on a retreat, at a church camp, or a festival service. Like Peter, we'd like to stay. But the moment of glory fades; the ordinary returns.

God may give us moments like that (we never have the right to demand them). We treasure them, remember them, and draw strength from them, but we can't hang on to them.

C. S. Lewis described it clearly in *Surprised by Joy:* "It is simply no good trying to keep any thrill; that is the very worst thing you can do. Let the thrill go—let it die away—go on through that period of death into the quieter interest and happiness that follow. And you will find that you are living in a world of new thrills all the time."

 Lord, I thank you for the times when I have experienced your presence. Let me be willing to leave the mountaintop and go back to the valley with you.

Recall a mountaintop experience you have had in prayer. If you feel ready to do so, share it with a friend in a conversation or letter.

■ FAITHFUL IN PRAYER

Rom. 12:9-21: "Be joyful in hope, patient in affliction, faithful in prayer" (v. 12).

We all need that encouragement to be "faithful in prayer," because we are tempted to quit for many reasons. We tell ourselves we are too busy. We pray only when we're in the mood. We begin to consider prayer optional. We grow impatient and think, "This doesn't work. This isn't doing any good." We may secretly dread the cost we will have to pay to make the prayer come true. An even deeper reason is our own unbelief, and behind that the grim face of the Evil One, who has a great stake in getting us to stop praying.

When we lapse into prayerlessness, there is only one solution: ask for God's forgiveness and start over. We need to overcome our moods by making prayer a matter of habit, by setting appointed times for prayer and then praying whether we feel like it or not.

The Quaker man of prayer Douglas Steere wrote: "The only really fatal failure is to stop praying and not to begin again."

 Lord of mercy, forgive my wavering commitment to the discipline of prayer. Help me begin again.

Today renew your commitment to remain faithful, with God's help, to this discipline of prayer.

■ THE SILENCE OF GOD

Psalm 22: "My God, my God, why have you forsaken me?" (v. 1).

There are times when we pray "out of the depths." We can summon up no faith, no religious emotions, no hope—only despair.

The psalm writer must have felt that kind of despair and forsakeness when he wrote Psalm 22. Jesus understands a prayer like this. In his loneliness and pain on the cross he made it his own (Matt. 27:46).

In such a moment of spiritual exhaustion all we are able to do is let go and feel ourselves drop, trusting that underneath are the everlasting arms. Like Jesus, we can pray, "Father, into your hands I commit my spirit" (Luke 23:46).

In his commentary on Matthew, William Barclay described the results of prayer of relinquishment like this: "Prayer does not remove the tragedy; it does not give us escape from the situation; it does not give us exemption from the task; but it does make us able to bear the unbearable; to face the unfaceable; to pass the breaking point and not break."

 Lord, into your hands I commit my spirit.

Do you have a friend or family member who is going through the depths? Is there something you can do today to "be with" them?

■ PRAY AND POST GUARD

Neh. 4:1-9:   "But we prayed to our God and posted a guard day and night to meet this threat" (v. 9).

After their long and weary exile in Babylon the people of Israel were set free to return to their own land. Spurred on by Nehemiah, they began to rebuild the walls of Jerusalem. This aroused the hostility of the pagans around them, who threatened to undo their work. The people of Israel took two essential steps: they prayed to God, and they posted a guard day and night.

Even as they prayed for God's protection and help, they did what they could. They knew that prayer is not a way to avoid responsibility, it is not a shortcut to success without effort.

Anthony Bloom gives this advice: "When we ask something in our prayers, we undertake by implication to do with all our strength, all our intelligence, and with all the courage and energy we have. In addition, we do it with all the power which God will give us. If we do not do this, we are wasting our time praying."

Lord of power and might, show me what I have to do and give me the strength to do it.

Reflect on these words of St. Augustine: "Without God we cannot; without us God will not."

■ WHATEVER YOU ASK

Mark 11:24: "Therefore I tell you, whatever you ask for in prayer, believe that you have received it, and it will be yours."

Do you remember Huck Finn's comments on prayer? "Miss Watson she took me in the closet and prayed, but nothing come of it. She told me to pray every day, and whatever I asked for I would get it. But it warn't so. I tried it. Once I got a fish-line, but no hooks. It warn't any good to me without hooks. I tried for the hooks three or four times, but somehow I couldn't make it work . . . . No, says I to myself, there ain't nothing in it."

We could laugh at Huck if he weren't so like ourselves. We can easily think of prayer as a way of getting something for ourselves, and then if it doesn't work after three or four times, we decide "there ain't nothing in it." Over and over we need to attach our faith to God and his promises.

In *Prayer* Hallesby wrote: "The power to believe *a promise* depends entirely on faith in *the one who made the promise.* Trust in the person arouses trust in his word. Only when we live with God in a personal, loving relationship where God himself is everything to us, only when our whole being is continually opened up and exposed to the mighty working of His holy presence within, is a capacity developed to believe that He gives whatever we ask."

 O God, I believe in you. Strengthen my faith in your promises.

Memorize today's key verse.

■ A STEP NEARER TO VICTORY

Luke 18:1-8: "Will not God bring about justice for his chosen ones, who cry out to him day and night?" (v. 7).

This is the second parable Jesus told urging us to "always pray and not give up."

Evil is firmly entrenched on the earth, and its victims are often the poor and powerless, like the widow in Jesus' story. Sometimes it takes a long time for God's poor, who cry day and night, to find justice. The mills of God grind slowly, but they do grind. Unjust leaders succeed for a time in setting up their hateful empires, but behind the scenes of history, God's justice is at work

James Russell Lowell declared this in a poem:

> *Truth forever on the scaffold,*
> *Wrong forever on the throne, —*
> *Yet that scaffold sways the future*
> *And, behind the dim unknown,*
> *Standeth God within the shadow,*
> *Keeping watch above his own.*

So we keep crying day and night—for justice in an unjust world, justice for ourselves and for all the poor and downtrodden, trusting that every prayer brings victory a step nearer.

 O Lord, let the cry for justice ring out day and night.

Choose one situation of injustice in the world and determine to pray about it until victory comes.

■ PRAYER AND ACTION

Luke 6:46-49: "Why do you call me 'Lord, Lord,' and do not do what I say?" (v. 46).

An old Hebrew legend says that when Moses struck the Red Sea with his staff, nothing happened. It was only when the first person plunged into the water that the sea was opened.

Often we have to act in order to release God's power. He will not do for us what we are perfectly capable of doing for ourselves. There's no use in praying, "Lord, Lord," if we are not willing to do what he says.

"Prayer is never the easy way out; never simply pushing things on God for him to do them for us," wrote William Barclay. "Prayer is power. It is not asking God to do something; it is asking him to make us able to do it ourselves."

We do not pray and then sit and wait. We pray and then rise and work. When we do, we find a new power entering our life.

 Lord, don't let me get away with using prayer as a dodge. Show me what I need to do, and give me the strength to do it.

Think of one thing you've been praying for. Is God waiting for you to take some action? Take one step in that direction today.

■ OUR FATHER

Matt. 6:5-15: "Our Father in heaven . . ." (v. 9).

When his disciples asked, "Lord, teach us to pray," Jesus taught them what we call the Lord's Prayer. We look at it now as an epitome of all we have learned about prayer.

Jesus taught us to pray to God as Father, even as *Abba*, the equivalent of *daddy*. Jesus' point is that God is like a kind and good parent. Human parents, even at their best, can be only a feeble imitation of the true parent we all need and want. Jesus encourages us to pray to God as our loving parent in heaven.

"Our Father" reminds us again that prayer is relationship. We pray to a God who is both personal and concerned. And we pray *our* Father—not *my* father. We pray it always as part of the largest family of all. Whatever we ask for ourselves we ask for God's children everywhere.

 Father, your name is Love. I'm grateful you are not a something, or even a someone, but the one who loves me more than anyone else.

As you pray the Lord's Prayer today, be conscious of the fact that you are praying it for and with all God's children.

■ HOLY NAME

Matt. 6:9-13:   "Hallowed be your name" (v. 9).

The prayer Jesus taught us begins with the things of
God. It first focuses our thoughts on our Father in
heaven, God's name, kingdom, and will.

We do not make God's name holy, but we pray that
it be hallowed with us. Perhaps this is the hardest
petition to translate into our 20th-century language.
God's *name* is God's nature and character, and we ask
that it be holy, special, and revered. We are praying,
"Let God be given the unique reverence he deserves
because of who God is. Let God be given first place in
our hearts."

Constance Garrett explained it this way in *Growth
in Prayer:* "We are praying that God's name be
reverenced and honored by all, but more particularly
by his own children. May we speak it only with
reverence; may we never say or do anything to bring
dishonor to God's name. May we, who bear his name,
hold it high and pure, untarnished by our carelessness
or forgetfulness. May the whole earth come to claim
him as Lord and Master."

When we pray this for someone else or for the
whole world, we pray that God would have the place
of honor in that life, in the life of our planet. It is
praying, "Let God be God."

 O God, I want you to have the place of honor
in my life—and in all the world.

**God has many names, each of which reveals some
aspect of God's character. What are your favorite
names for God?**

■ THE COMING OF THE KINGDOM

Matt. 6:10: "Your kingdom come."

This petition looks in three directions. In a sense the kingdom has already come. When Jesus began his ministry, he announced that the kingdom of God was near. God's rule came in a special way as Jesus taught, healed the sick, fed the hungry, and liberated people from the powers of evil. The kingdom continues to come now, wherever God's ruling power is extended in our lives. And we look to the future to the time when the kingdom is fully come.

To pray for the kingdom to come is to pray that we ourselves, our whole society, and our whole world accepts God as King. Our ultimate allegiance is not to any national government, but to God's kingdom. This petition then is our pledge of allegiance to the kingdom of God.

This is a large petition indeed. In it we are praying for peace, for justice, for a world order in which none need be hungry or terror-stricken or oppressed. This petition will not be fully answered until "at the name of Jesus every knee should bow . . . and every tongue confess that Jesus Christ is Lord, to the glory of God the Father" (Phil. 2:10-11).

 Lord, bring in your kingdom, beginning with me.

What would it mean for God's kingdom to come in your life? In your community? In our nation? In the world?

■ YOUR WILL BE DONE

Matt. 6:10:   "Your will be done on earth as it is in heaven."

This petition closely parallels the previous one. God's kingdom comes when God's will is done; as God's will is done, the kingdom of God is extended.

Prayer is a mighty power not for getting our will done in heaven, but for getting God's will done here on earth. We are praying not, "God, your will be changed," but "your will be done."

At times this is a prayer of submission, because there are always things we cannot change. Though God may not have sent them, God has permitted them to come. So like Jesus in the Garden, we pray, "Your will, not mine."

But this petition is also a commitment to action. We are asking that we be enabled to do God's will. In *Letters to Malcolm* C. S. Lewis wrote: "Taken this way, I find the words have a more regular daily application. For there isn't always—or we don't always have reason to suspect that there is—some great affliction looming in the near future, but there are always duties to be done; usually, for me, neglected duties to be caught up with. 'Thy will be *done*—by me—now' brings me back to brass tacks."

 "God grant me the serenity to accept the things I cannot change, courage to change the things I can, and wisdom to know the difference."

What is God asking you to do today? Get back to "brass tacks"!

■ DAILY BREAD

Matt. 6:11: "Give us today our daily bread."

Having first raised our eyes to God and to God's name, kingdom, and will, we then pray for our own needs. The petition for daily bread reminds us of several important truths.

God is the source of all good things. We are dependent on the Creator for everything we need, and he has promised to provide it.

God cares about our physical needs, and so it is proper for us to pray for them.

We pray for bread, not cake. God has promised to meet all our needs, but not all our requests. In God's goodness we are given much more than necessities, but we have no right to expect luxuries while others need bread.

This petition too is prayed in the plural. Around the world today hungry people are praying, "Give us today our daily bread." God may want to answer their prayer through you.

We pray only for what we need for this day. The petition also teaches us to live one day at a time.

 Gracious Lord, I dare to ask for all I need, but only for what I need, and just enough for this day.

As a commentary on this petition read Matthew 6:19-34.

■ FORGIVE AS WE FORGIVE

Matt. 6:12-15: "Forgive us our debts, as we also have forgiven our debtors" (v. 12).

Andrew Murray wrote: "As bread is the first need of the body, so forgiveness is for the soul." The Bible has many words for sin. Here sin is pictured as debts, something we owe to God. This points especially to our sins of omission, the never-ending story of good left undone, our sins of procrastination and irresolution and neglect.

This is the only petition that Jesus elaborates on. He does it to state in the strongest possible terms that we dare not expect God's forgiveness if we are unwilling to offer it to others.

Our ability to forgive others is based on the knowledge that God has forgiven us. If I have been hurt deeply by another, it may not be easy to forgive. It may help us to remember that forgiving is not a matter of feelings; it is a matter of the will. Are you willing to forgive—or at the least, are you willing to be made willing? We can ask God to change our hearts. We can by an act of will say, "I forgive." The feelings will probably follow, but even if they do not, we have done the right thing.

 O God of mercy, I know that you have cancelled my debts. Help me forgive anyone who owes me.

Is there someone you need to forgive today? Do it now, in your heart, and if it seems right, by word or letter.

■ DO NOT BRING US TO THE TEST

Matt. 6:13:   "And lead us not into temptation."

The word *temptation* here may be a problem for us, because we usually think of something that draws us into sin. God, of course, does not tempt us in that sense. Perhaps the meaning of this petition comes out more clearly in the translation, "Do not bring us to the test." We are asking, "Don't let us get into a situation that is too much for us." "Don't let something happen that we can't handle." "Deliver us from evil so great that it is more than we can cope with."

We are praying that God will give us the sense and fortitude to stay out of situations that would strain our resolve to the breaking point.

In the larger sense this is a prayer for the defeat of all forces and customs in our society that corrupt both young and old. It is a prayer for a righteous society.

 Lord, do not bring us to the test. Save us from the time of trial.

Do you know someone who is in a time of trial? Today pray the Lord's Prayer for that person.

■ DELIVER US

Matt. 6:13:   "Deliver us from the evil one."

The Bible is a thoroughly realistic book. It does not pretend that all is for the best in the best of all possible worlds. It knows that there are other forces at work in opposition to God. This world is not a playground but a battlefield. Because of these powers of evil, personified in the evil one, we can speak of prayer as spiritual warfare. One reason our prayers are not always answered immediately or perfectly is because of these entrenched powers of evil.

The Christian belief is that by his life, death, and resurrection Jesus won the decisive battle against evil. The war goes on, but victory is assured.

Again, we pray this petition for deliverance not just for ourselves, but for the whole human family. This is another large petition—against war, corruption, greed—against all that opposes God.

 Deliver us from all evil, O Lord.

For a good novel about the battle against evil, read C. S. Lewis's *That Hideous Strength* (Macmillan, 1947).

■ FOR EVER

Matt. 6:13:   "For yours is the kingdom and the power and the glory forever."

We have only sampled the riches of meaning that lie in this magnificent prayer. It's one of those "simple" prayers that a child can be taught to pray, but as we ponder its meaning day by day, our understanding of it will grow until it encompasses everything God offers us and asks us.

In some Bible manuscripts the Lord's Prayer ends with the doxology or words of praise: "For yours is the kingdom and the power and the glory forever." This closes the prayer on a note of adoration—moving our thoughts beyond ourselves and our problems to God's eternal kingdom and power and glory. The doxology points us beyond history to the great moment when everything is gathered up into God, when we will join the redeemed of all time in praying, "Amen! Praise and glory and wisdom and thanks and honor and power and strength be to our God for ever and ever. Amen!" (Rev. 7:12).

Thine is the kingdom; unto thee
Shall bow in homage ev'ry knee.
And thine the pow'r, no pow'r shall be
That is not overcome by thee.
The glory thine; by ev'ry tongue
Thy praise shall be forever sung!

What is the next step on your pilgrimage of prayer?

AFTERWORD

You have now completed your journey of a hundred days. You have reflected on important biblical words about prayer, and you have experimented with different ways of praying. You have gone a long way toward establishing a firm habit of prayer.

Where do you go from here? Let me make just a few suggestions.

1. Continue to make prayer a part of your regular schedule. Assign time to it.

2. Begin your time of prayer by reading from the Bible and other spiritual books.

3. Try for balance in your prayer life—between pattern and freedom, between written prayers and spontaneous ones.

4. Include the various types of prayer. I follow the ACTS formula: A—Adoration or praise, C—Confession, T—Thanksgiving, S—Supplication (prayers for myself and others). I try to include some of each kind in my regular time of prayer.

5. Use brief moments to "practice the presence of God," and to pray without ceasing.

6. Go back over the book and look at the suggested actions. If there are some that were especially meaningful for you, think of how you can continue to include them in your daily routine.

7. Don't go it alone. If you can, pray with others in a small group as well as in the public worship of the church. We all need that enrichment and support.

BIBLIOGRAPHY

Bloesch, Donald. *The Struggle of Prayer.* San
   Francisco: Harper & Row, 1980.
Bloom, Anthony. *Beginning to Pray.* New York:
   Paulist, 1970.
Bonhoeffer, Dietrich. *Life Together.* New York:
   Harper & Row, 1954.
Brother Lawrence. *Practicing the Presence of God.*
   Available in many editions.
Evely, Louis. *The Prayer of a Modern Man.* Wilkes-
   Barre, Pa.: Dimension Books, 1968.
Garrett, Constance. *Growth in Prayer.* New York:
   Macmillan, 1950.
Hallesby, O. *Prayer.* Minneapolis: Augsburg, 1931.
Kelly, Thomas. *Testament of Devotion.* New York:
   Harper & Row, 1941.
Kelsey, Morton. *The Other Side of Silence: A Guide to
   Christian Meditation.* New York: Paulist, 1976.
Klug, Ronald. *How to Keep a Spiritual Journal.* New
   York: Thomas Nelson, 1982.
Laubach, Frank. *Prayer: The Mightiest Force in the
   World.* Old Tappan, N.J.: Fleming H. Revell, 1946.
Leech, Kenneth. *True Prayer.* San Francisco: Harper
   & Row, 1980.
Lewis, C. S. *Letters.* London: Geoffrey Bles, 1966.

Lewis, C. S. *Letters to Malcolm: Chiefly on Prayer*. New York: Harcourt, Brace & World, 1964.

Lewis, C. S. *Surprised by Joy*. New York: Harcourt, Brace, 1955.

Lewis, C. S. *The World's Last Night*. New York: Harcourt, Brace, 1960.

Lewis, C. S., ed. *George Macdonald: An Anthology*. New York: Macmillan, 1978.

Maclachlan, Lewis. *The Teaching of Jesus on Prayer*. London: James Clark, 1952.

Murray, Andrew. *The Believer's School of Prayer*. Minneapolis: Bethany House, 1982. A new edition of *With Christ in the School of Prayer* (1885).

Von Zeller, Dom Hubert. *Prayer in Other Words*. Springfield, Ill.: Templegate, 1963.

Weatherhead, Leslie. *A Private House of Prayer*. Nashville: Abingdon, 1958.